Healing
the
Sensitive
Hert

How to stop getting hurt,
build your inner strength,
and find the love you deserve

Debra Mandel, Ph.D.

Adams Media Corporation
Avon, Massachusetts

Published by
Adams Media Corporation
57 Littlefield Street, Avon MA 02322. U.S.A.
www.adamsmedia.com

ISBN: 1-58062-708-0

Printed in Canada.

J I H G F E D C B

Library of Congress Cataloging-in-Publication Data
Mandel, Debra.
Healing the sensitive heart / by Debra Mandel.
p. cm.
ISBN 1-58062-708-0
1. Psychological abuse. 2. Adult child abuse victims. 3. Sensitivity
(Personality trait) 4. Interpersonal relations. 5. Psychic trauma.
6. Distress (Psychology) 7. Self-actualization (Psychology) I. Title.
RC569.5.P75 M36 2003
616.85'82--dc21
2002011334

This publication is designed to provide accurate and authoritative information with regard to the subject matter covered. It is sold with the understanding that the publisher is not engaged in rendering legal, accounting, or other professional advice. If legal advice or other expert assistance is required, the services of a competent professional person should be sought.
—From a *Declaration of Principles* jointly adopted by a Committee of the American Bar Association and a Committee of Publishers and Associations

Disclaimer
In order to protect the anonymity and privacy of my clients, I have changed their names, circumstances, and other identifying information. Any similarity to actual people is coincidental. In some cases, I've created composites that closely resemble the experiences of real people.

The information in this book is meant to educate, illustrate, and offer hope to people with sensitive hearts and their loved ones. It is in no way intended to be a replacement for professional help.

Cover illustration by Kathie Kelleher.

This book is available at quantity discounts for bulk purchases.
For information, call 1-800-872-5627.

DEDICATION

To all sensitive-hearted souls: May you find the
hope and strength to mend your wounds, cherish
your gift of emotions, and transform your pain
into the treasure that will help you thrive.

♥ ♥ ♥ ♥ ♥ ♥ ♥ ♥ ♥

ACKNOWLEDGMENTS

I wish to thank my precious daughter, Tiffany, for being exactly
who she is. Because of her, I've learned more about love and
forgiveness than I ever have in any relationship. Just when I
thought I had healed most of the wounds beneath my own sensitive heart, she came along and I discovered my healing path
had only just begun. I will forever be grateful to have her in my
life and for all the windows she has unknowingly opened for me
to explore. Her caring and trusting nature teaches me just how
vulnerable children can be and how parents need to protect
their sensitive hearts. I hope my daughter will always know how
important she is to my life and how she serves as an endless
source of inspiration for me to stay on my healing path. She is
truly a treasure to behold.

I wish to thank my dear friend Jon, who weathered all of
my anxieties and insecurities about becoming a writer. His dedication to standing by my side through each written and
rewritten word continues to amaze and astound me. Were it not
for his care and support and continual pouring-out of encouragement, I would never have gotten this far.

I wish to thank my family, my parents, and my two wonderful nieces. Special thanks to my sister, Cheryl. While we have
certainly gone head-to-head with our differences, I've grown to
trust her love and care for me. Special thanks to my father, who,
in spite of his not understanding much about emotional healing,
has taken the time and energy to work toward mending our
relationship. Though the pain has often overwhelmed us both,

for today, it all seems worth the struggle no matter how difficult it's been. And, special thanks to my stepmother, Dora, for her kind words of support.

I wish to thank my agent, Carol Susan Roth, for believing in my talent as a writer and helping me persevere through many rejections, changes, and disappointments. Though we have not always been in sync with formulating the ideas for this book, she continually demonstrated respect and sensitivity for my creative endeavors.

I wish to thank my wonderful friends who have believed in me even when I couldn't hold onto my own worth. Through these precious relationships, I've become more able to see the mirror of positive energy they reflect back to me.

I wish to express my deepest gratitude for all the sensitive-hearted souls who have shared their stories, pain, and suffering with me in psychotherapy. Each has helped me stay in touch with compassion, hope, and strength. I thank all of them for trusting me with their vulnerabilities. Were it not for these gifted and special people, there would be no book. With each story expressed, the door opens to allow someone else to be helped.

I wish to also thank my editor, Claire Gerus, whose encouraging feedback helped erase many of my doubts about pursuing such a creative challenge. Taking on a new writer requires faith, and I'm ever so fortunate that she could envision my success and go to bat for me to get a contract.

I wish to thank all of the intimate partners I've been fortunate to share experiences with. Though endings have often been unbearably painful (as of course they would be for a sensitive heart), I've been blessed with many gifts from each encounter and wouldn't trade any of them to have avoided the pain. So my deepest thanks to all whom I've loved and all who have shared their love with me. Last, but ever so important, I wish to thank Chris for allowing my vision of a healthy-hearted relationship to become a reality.

♥ CONTENTS ♥

INTRODUCTION

I have a special affinity for those with sensitive hearts. As far back as I can remember, I've been a magnet for vulnerable creatures, from birds with broken wings to homeless kittens to people with broken hearts. At first I thought I was cursed to be surrounded by such pain and suffering, but later I learned to see my own sensitivity as a precious treasure and grew to cherish it. Helping people with their hurts was my gift. As a psychologist with over nineteen years of experience, I have worked with hundreds of souls whose hearts have become extra sensitive. Just a few examples . . .

- Betty's father constantly criticized her appearance, calling her fat and forever commenting on her flaws. Her mother put her on diets and told her to stop upsetting her father. Betty learned to hate her body, mistrust men, and fear intimacy. She married a womanizer who had an affair, told her it was her fault, and then left her with their two children.
- Philip's mother was depressed and often self-absorbed. She would holler at Philip when frustration got the best of her. Philip grew to feel inadequate and undeserving of love. He married the first woman who showed any interest, but she withdrew whenever Philip asked anything of her.
- When Jane's parents decided to divorce, she became the target of a nasty custody battle. As an adult, Jane constantly sought out relationships with high levels of drama and conflict. She took a job as executive assistant to a man infamous for screaming at his subordinates and making their lives miserable.
- Susan learned to be a meticulous housekeeper to ward off her mother's criticism. After marrying Bob, Susan continued

to clean compulsively, believing he would be angry if her cleanliness lapsed even a bit. But Bob would have preferred that they relax, order in a pizza, watch television, and make love. He had no idea of Susan's panic whenever she was not cleaning house.

- Don keeps others at such a distance that he never allows himself to feel close to anyone. His parents had a complete lack of regard for his privacy needs and refused to trust him, despite his being an honor student and a very well-behaved, respectful boy. They eavesdropped on his phone conversations with friends and constantly went through his drawers looking for drugs, even though he had truly given them no reason to be suspicious. By the time Don reached adulthood, he viewed the world as invasive and violating. He guarded his right to privacy with such vigor that he missed out on enjoying the benefits of social relationships.

- After her fourth unsuccessful long-term relationship, Cathy was convinced that she attracted every guy who didn't like women and was resigned that this was her destiny in life. She absolutely believed that her relationships *chose* her. Because of this conviction, Cathy never even saw the option to not get involved in the first place, even when she came face to face with red flags.

- Tom's mother threatened to send him to boarding school whenever he failed to follow her instructions. As an adult, Tom always imagined the worst. He feared he would lose his job if he ever made a mistake. Eventually his fears came true when his boss fired him. Tom's work was excellent, but none of his co-workers wanted to have anything to do with him. "He's such a pessimist!" they would say.

- Ruth believed she was a burden to the world. Whenever she needed something, even from her best friends, she was convinced that others would be angry and perceive her to be a problem. Even when greeted with her friends' love and support, Ruth would still search for the unspoken hostility she "knew" was there, in the exact same way she had learned to cope with her resentful parents, by trying to anticipate their reactions.

- John became enraged whenever he had to stand in line, even for events he looked forward to attending. He desperately wanted immediate gratification because of how long he had been required to wait as a child to get any of his needs met. Many times, he got no response at all to his needs; other times, his parents responded but treated his needs as a burden. As an adult, John transferred his expectations onto the world at large. He believed his demands were reasonable and couldn't understand why the world repeatedly disappointed him. At the same time, the expectations he had of his significant relationships were far too low.

Each of these people came to me because they felt trapped by events in their past, their own vulnerability, and their powerlessness to create the love they so desperately needed. Unfortunately, their condition is all too common. People with sensitive hearts come in all shapes and sizes. Some carry severe emotional wounds, others have milder reminders. Some have suffered horrible forms of child abuse, leaving the deepest of scars. Others have endured less overt persecution but share the experience of having been victimized nevertheless.

I've discovered that the important thing is not whether a child was actually mistreated; what matters is whether the child *felt* wounded by his or her circumstances. And far too many of us fall into that category. For example, Alice was never hit, molested, or neglected by her parents. She received adequate clothing, shelter, and other physical necessities. She even went on family vacations. But to Alice, something very deep was missing. She didn't get attention, praise, hugs, acknowledgment of her talents, or even a pat on the back for major achievements.

While the treatment Alice received wasn't all that bad—it was actually pretty good, relative to what many of her friends experienced—her adult behavior was that of a person whose childhood history screamed of blatant mistreatment.

While sensitive-hearted individuals often develop extremely effective coping skills as children, the same beliefs and behaviors are less successful when it comes to dealing with adult life. That's because they've entrenched themselves in a self-protective shield. They're so busy protecting their bruised hearts that they shut themselves off from many of the best things in life. They usually expect less, and, more often than not, they receive less than they deserve. They find themselves suffering from chronic disappointment, resentment, disillusionment, and anger. They often experience addictions, eating disorders, depression, anxiety, financial and job difficulties, and, without a doubt, problems in relationships. These people are typically magnets for more pain, unconsciously seeking out relationships that will once again prompt them to feel the anguish and torment from their original wounds.

Though people with sensitive hearts differ in their symptoms, they have a great deal in common.

- They believe they are powerless, without choices, and out of control.
- They take on responsibility for things they cannot control, like other people's actions. At the same time, they have trouble taking ownership of things they do control—like their own behavior, thoughts, and feelings.
- They do not know how to decline the unrealistic demands of others, and they may feel shame or guilt if they do.
- They live in fear of other people's negative reactions and often doubt their own perception of reality.

- They engage with people who treat them badly, and they stay far too long in situations or relationships where they feel trapped and mistreated.
- People with sensitive hearts often mistreat their bodies, indulging in destructive behaviors like alcohol or drug abuse, binge eating, overwork, and so on.
- They diminish their self-value by repeating in their heads all of the negative messages they learned from important caregivers, other influential people, or the media or culture at large.

People with sensitive hearts usually have little (if any) awareness of how they re-create situations and relationships that make them relive the pain and suffering they endured as children. They do not recognize that, as adults, they have *choices* about the people they pick for social and intimate relationships. As a result, they usually perpetuate their lousy relationships time after time, then wonder why there are no good men or women out there or why they are just so unlucky. Some may have even created positive relationships, but, like Susan (the compulsive cleaner), they're unable to experience the good things those relationships bring to their lives.

If you believe yourself to be caught in the vicious cycle of re-creating old wounds, take heart! The human spirit is astoundingly resilient, regardless of the level of wound. In nearly two decades of clinical practice, I have seen hundreds of sensitive-hearted souls transform themselves into healthy-hearted individuals with bright futures and joyful days. Based upon my work with these courageous people, I have created an extremely effective process to help them heal. The process first allows them to acknowledge the pain of their past, then to recognize how old patterns are running (and often ruining) their relationships. After discovering the unique gifts their experiences have given them, they are able to create new ways of believing and acting that will help them get the love they want so much.

You may not believe me now, but you have tremendous potential power. As a therapist, I've seen that, despite the deepest of wounds, there are extraordinary rewards, like the soldier whose suffering earns a Purple Heart.

- You possess compassion and empathy more far-reaching than that of people who have never suffered.
- You have the healing power to help others in your same boat.
- You can handle life's hardships with greater endurance and stamina.
- You can reach the richest form of intimacy without losing your *self*.

Sounds pretty good, doesn't it? In the chapters that follow, you'll discover an abundance of new tools and ways to view the world. All your discoveries will help you develop the two most important components of a healthy heart: a nurturing relationship with yourself and the opportunity to have the deepest, most loving relationships with others. This book isn't about toughening a bruised or sensitive heart; openness and vulnerability are vital in creating truly deep relationships. You will learn an essential skill. You will learn how to share all of your heart and your emotions from a place of wholeness, where strength coexists with vulnerability; love is supported by appropriate rules and boundaries; and eagerness and intelligence go hand in hand when it comes to approaching others. Most of all, you'll discover what it means to have a healthy-hearted relationship with every aspect of yourself—the most important relationship any of us can have. Like Betty, Tom, Ruth, and the others, you will reclaim your inherent right to thrive!

Chapter One

Is Your Heart Sensitive?

At every level of society, millions of women and men feel as if they've been wounded to the heart—to their emotional cores. Their hearts become *sensitive*, not in the sense of emotional openness but more like the way a bruise is tender—a spot that's been hit again and again. People with sensitive hearts are not simply born with more "emotional genes." Most often, this kind of tenderness or sensitivity arises because these people feel they have been harmed, betrayed, and bewildered by others, both personally and professionally. Old, painful experiences and relationships have stunted their emotional lives.

People with sensitive hearts become trapped in toxic emotional patterns, continually drawing into their lives individuals who eventually hurt, disappoint, or frustrate them. They find themselves being mistreated over and over again until it becomes the only way of life they know. They are unfulfilled in their personal and professional relationships, hurting emotionally, misunderstood, and often hopeless. They are seemingly doomed to a habitual pattern of repeated unsuccessful relationships, causing frustration, sadness, even despair. And since there has been no way to aptly describe this chronic and debilitating condition, most of these sufferers have no idea of what's happening to them.

While feelings of vulnerability can be triggered by events at every stage of life, the deepest, most painful sensitivities of the heart usually originate in youth. In childhood we are all naturally open and vulnerable. Unfortunately, that means our hearts are wounded very easily. Parents may neglect, ignore, or criticize their sons and daughters; some may even go so far as to beat, molest, degrade, or humiliate them. Teachers and peers call children names, bully them, or assert unnecessarily harsh control. Even a well-intended correction or joke can create an emotional wound if a child is by nature more vulnerable or emotionally fragile. Whether the mistreatment is overt or subtle, physical, psychological, or emotional, real or imagined, children can grow into adulthood with feelings of having been hurt. Even when they minimize their history, believe they deserved what they got, or live in complete denial about it, many harbor deep wounds from the past.

SALLY'S STORY

Sally was at her wits' end. She hadn't slept for days. Disappointed with life, she had closed herself off from the support of her friends. She was having a hard time functioning at work and couldn't get herself interested in the things she typically enjoyed. Yet she would not succumb to her depression. She perceived herself as a survivor with a strong life force.

As we talked about her life, we saw many connections between unresolved pain from her childhood and the distress she often felt in her adult intimate relationships with men. Sally's mother and father had divorced when Sally was ten. Her parents had constantly bickered and demonstrated a general dislike for one another. Although at times they attempted to shield their children from their problems, their anger often erupted into hostile outbreaks where they just couldn't help themselves from shouting openly, despite their recognition of the potential damage to their children.

After the divorce, Sally saw her father fairly regularly. But he often seemed indifferent and distant, and she never felt close to him. He remarried two years later to a woman with two children of her own. Though Sally's stepmother tried to include her in the new family, Sally couldn't help but feel displaced by her stepsiblings. As years passed, her father became less interested in Sally's life and far more involved with his new family.

Sally's mother did the best she could raising Sally and her other two children. Despite good intentions, however, she lacked the emotional and financial resources to adequately care for their needs. She was always "borrowing" money, food, and clothing with promises of repaying the debt, but she never seemed to get ahead enough to do so. Because she felt so needy herself, she never even passed these goodies on to her children. To make matters worse, Sally heard constantly about her mother's suffering and how Sally's father had wronged her.

When Sally's mother became particularly stressed, she would blame the kids for demanding too much of her, even though all they wanted was regular kid stuff like toys and bikes, and, of course, the full range of emotional supplies like attention, affection, acknowledgment, and praise. Unfortunately, all was in short supply. Sally internalized an image of herself as a burden, undeserving of having her basic needs met.

Sally had no one to talk to. Not even her two older siblings were as bothered by the family experience. Sally grew to believe she was too sensitive and that she should keep her feelings to herself. Secretly, she longed to have her father return home so things would be "normal" again, but she recognized that this would never happen. Despite his relative absence in her life after the divorce, she held onto a glorified image of him.

Not surprisingly, when Sally left home at nineteen, she was underequipped to create healthy, intimate relationships. Her mother remained bitter, dating only sporadically with no expectation of ever finding love in her life. And while her father seemed happy with his wife, Sally felt displaced, not good enough for her father's love. Sally had never witnessed a loving relationship devoid of pain and suffering. She lacked self-worth.

While Sally dated many different kinds of men as a young woman, all her relationships had something in common. They all began with flowers, expensive gifts, fancy dates, and promises of care, but each degenerated into long nights of quarreling, hostility, and disrespect for differences of opinion. Each time Sally was left with the sense that she was unloved, unlovable, and an intolerable burden. She was so frightened of being abandoned and left alone that she convinced herself to stay even when she noticed her own unhappiness in these relationships, believing she would never find anyone who would truly love her.

Sally seemed unaware of the degree of pain she had experienced in childhood and the resulting damage to her emotional well-being. "No biggie, I'm sure everybody has had these kinds of experiences," she said and shrugged. She was unable to see the connections between her current problems and her childhood wounds. She vowed that she would never have the kind of relationship her parents had, but she lacked the information and healing to be able to prevent this re-creation.

She thought she had picked a good man in Bob, her latest boyfriend, because he at least told her he loved her. Yet his actions continually contradicted his statements. He constantly flirted with other women, preferred to be out with the guys until the wee hours, and wouldn't make any commitments beyond the next day. If Sally complained, he told her she was overreacting and that she had better not try to change him or he'd leave her. He wouldn't be accountable for his behavior. Sally blamed herself when he ended the relationship. She even believed her requests for respect and kindness were unreasonable.

Sally felt victimized in many of her relationships. After each, she swore that she would not allow herself to be mistreated ever again. Like many people who feel victimized and survive, she mistook her rage for empowerment. Sometimes this faulty thinking led to destructive behavior, in which she would alienate potentially positive people from getting close to her. At times, she would even unconsciously pick fights with people who were capable of really hurting her physically.

Sally was starved for connection, but her choice of friends and associates was poor. She picked people who were happy to take advantage of her kindness. She didn't know how to assert her needs, so she showered people with surprise gifts and unasked-for acts of generosity. Having depleted her few emotional and financial resources, she then couldn't find anyone to help her replenish them. She constantly put more into social relationships than she got back, then wondered why people betrayed her.

Sally's story illustrates the havoc of an unhealed heart. Bruised by the behavior of those who were supposed to be taking care of her as a child, Sally exhibited many of the behaviors and beliefs adopted by the emotionally wounded in order to cope with a less than ideal world. More importantly, her story demonstrates the real peril of an impermeable self-protective shield. While the shield aims to provide shelter from further pain, in actuality it creates a vicious cycle. Sensitive-hearted people re-create and repeat the same destructive patterns of childhood in their adult relationships.

Sally touched my heart in every way. That first day in therapy I wanted to cuddle her, soothe all her hurt away, tell her it would be all right, and fix everything for her. Beneath her sophisticated and proud veneer, I sensed a starving child, and I wanted to feed her emotionally and spiritually. However, I could also tell she wasn't going to accept comfort easily as her shield kept her out of reach. I would have to earn her respect and trust.

I proposed that Sally and I enter into an agreement. Together, we would do the hard work of recognizing and developing the strengths she had already demonstrated. She would first have to recall and heal the sadness and hurt of her past and then change her behavior and beliefs in the present to meet the challenges of health and sanity. She would have to be willing to let go of an emotionally destructive way of life and entertain the possibility of nurturing connections. To earn Sally's trust, I had to share my observations and resources candidly yet warmly. I needed to demonstrate empathy and compassion to avoid any chance that she might feel shamed. Sometimes I needed to confront her when I thought she was in denial; sometimes I needed to just soothe her when her pain became unbearable. All the while, I tried to offer consistency, honesty, and hope.

Sally needed to see that she had actually been *enriched* by her experiences, not damaged or broken. She needed to come to recognize and embrace the power and strength she possessed. I needed to provide the lens through which she could envision a far wider realm of possibilities.

In my nineteen years of clinical practice, I have worked with many people who've suffered like Sally did, as well as others who suffered much more blatant harm or neglect or different versions of it. Some have even had what might be called a "normal" childhood, yet somehow their hearts became extra sensitive anyway. I've seen what can happen when wounds from the past and their resulting sensitivities are healed and new emotional and behavioral patterns created.

Sensitive-hearted people possess enormous resources and strengths. When they learn to use these assets, real transformation becomes truly possible. In Sally's case, one of her resources was a considerable talent for art, and expressing that artistic side became an essential part of her healing. For several years, Sally had dabbled in crafts and taken courses in ceramics and drawing at night school. As her therapy progressed, she began to make highly sophisticated collages, which expressed (sometimes directly, sometimes abstractly) the pain she had been through. She plans to earn a teaching credential and teach art to children.

Today, Sally is working as a waitress to support herself while in school. She takes as many or as few classes as she can handle, and she has begun to sell her artwork. Sally's collage making has kept her hopeful about the many wonderful opportunities she can create for herself. She now delights in her own "kookiness" and cherishes her idiosyncratic approach to existence.

The process of healing has not been easy. Sally had hoped she could put her memories into a package and forget them. Instead, her job was to actively retrieve and revisit them, not through the eyes of the wounded child, but from the eyes of a resourceful and competent adult. She has had to forgive herself, to recognize and eliminate coping behaviors that no longer serve her, and deal with the feelings of self-doubt and inadequacy she has avoided for so long. And then the biggest, most difficult step: she has had to declare her own worthiness to love and be loved.

As she developed a sense of her own value and found herself succeeding at work, in school, and in her art, Sally's relationships improved. She now attracts people who reciprocate her acts of kindness. She even enjoys receiving from others. She met a man she is now dating. She feels liked and respected by the people she socializes with. She no longer wishes to hide from the world.

Sally wakes up excited by the day's prospects. She no longer copes and just gets by. Sally would be the first to admit that her life is at times difficult, but the challenges no longer debilitate her. Sally no longer identifies herself as a "survivor" with a bruised heart. Rather, she has become a "Thriver." As a Thriver, Sally is finally free to grow and blossom into the wonderful human being she truly is. Thrivers, like Sally, welcome life's challenges. They're optimistic and enthusiastic about the world.

♥ ♥ ♥ ♥ ♥ ♥ ♥ ♥ ♥

I have dedicated my professional practice to helping people just like Sally, and those with far more grueling histories, heal their sensitive hearts and become healthy-hearted again. Healthy-hearted individuals do no lose their sensitivity. Rather, their sensitivity becomes a resource that can be embraced and cherished.

The bruises heal and the self becomes stronger and even more resilient. If you picked up this book, you probably have at least some recognition that you may have a sensitive heart, with hurts that keep you from living your life to the fullest. You may feel there's something missing in your relationships, or maybe you feel that the world has treated you harshly. Your personal history may be like Sally's, or it might be more or less traumatic. Regardless of the events of your life, you may feel bruised or emotionally tender when it comes to being in the world.

Many people with sensitive hearts go through years of therapy, only to end up calling themselves "survivors." "I survived my childhood," they'll say, or "I survived a traumatic relationship." But I believe there is a level of living far beyond mere survival. It's what I call Thriver living, when your mind and emotions fully support healthy, happy relationships. When you thrive, you can look back at your emotional wounds and recognize the gifts they have given you. You are free of old patterns of feeling, believing, and acting that no longer serve you. Most importantly, you can choose the way you approach life every single minute. Instead of being emotionally clenched, looking to deflect the next blow, you can welcome the people and relationships in your life as enriching experiences rather than as potential sources of pain.

Remember Betty, who grew up hating her body? Now she enjoys the bumps and curves of her body. She works for a rising Internet company, and she dates men who treat her with caring and respect. Philip, divorced from his first wife, now enjoys life with a loving partner. They share household chores, make decisions together, and discuss problems openly. Susan's house isn't quite as clean because she's focusing more on what will truly make both her and her husband, Bob, happy. They order a lot more pizza—and have a lot more fun!

Tom and Jane have learned to create better relationships at work, filling their own needs while adding greatly to the team environment at their respective companies. Ruth and John understand how unrealistic their expectations of their friends were, and now their relationships with others are focused on giving and receiving on an equal, supportive basis.

All of these people have discovered how it feels to relate in a healthy-hearted way to themselves and to the world. They have escaped the binds of their past emotional wounds, and instead of surviving, they are thriving. Sure, things still arise; other people may still create emotional upheaval in the lives of the formerly heart-sensitive. But these now healthy-hearted souls relate to these wounds very differently. They know what they themselves create and what others are responsible for. They take responsibility for what they can change and let the rest go. They finally understand how much the world can offer us when we approach it with an open hand instead of a clenched fist. They have actively stepped out of the trap of their old emotional wounds, and now they can stand free and clear, with healthy hearts.

If you feel your heart is sensitive because of wounds in your past, or if you are simply dissatisfied with the relationships you have created time and time again, I encourage you to take the following test to evaluate your level of sensitivity. Then read this book and put its processes to work for you. Remember, emotional wounds come in all shapes, sizes, and degrees; like a skinned knee, it's better to take good care of the small hurts so they don't turn into something more serious. And if your emotional wounds truly cut to the core of your sensitive heart, this book can help you heal at the deepest possible level, allowing you to experience the joy and freedom of a truly thriving life.

TAKE THE TEST: AT WHAT LEVEL IS YOUR HEART SENSITIVE?

After treating hundreds of people with sensitive hearts, I've developed the following exam to help identify the major indicators. By providing a detailed overview and familiar points of reference, the results of this test can serve as a valuable tool in helping discover if you—or someone you love—continues to suffer the havoc of an unhealed bruised heart.

Don't be surprised if you identify with many or even most of these questions. Emotional wounds are found in every state, region, and family group; the process of becoming heart-sensitive shows no favoritism to intelligence, creativity, gender, race, or social class. Read the following twenty-five questions, and choose the response that best describes how you feel most of the time. Then add up your total score.

Never (0 points)   Frequently (3 points)
Seldom (1 point)   Always (4 points)
Sometimes (2 points)

Give yourself a 0, 1, 2, 3, or 4 according to your answer to each question.

____ 1. Do you feel unloved?
____ 2. Do you feel undeserving of things you want?
____ 3. Are you dissatisfied with the way you are treated in your close relationships?
____ 4. Do you feel you were abused in childhood by any of the following: family, other caregivers, peer group, cultural prejudices, or sexism?
____ 5. Do you treat yourself destructively by eating too much or not enough, through alcohol or drugs, overspending, gambling, excessive exercise, or any other mechanism?
____ 6. Do you feel powerless or out of control?
____ 7. Do you get annoyed or scared when you discover you have different feelings, reactions, or thoughts from people close to you?
____ 8. Do you feel you stay in situations that may be hurting you or where you cut others too much slack?

___ 9. Do you avoid situations where you may experience unwanted feelings like fear, anger, sadness, or even happiness in order to appear "together" or "strong"?

___ 10. Do you feel shame?

___ 11. Do you take responsibility for things that have little or nothing to do with you?

___ 12. Do you censor your opinions or feelings for fear of being put down, attacked, or criticized by either friends, relatives, or strangers?

___ 13. Do you go out of your way to be nice to people even when you're angry with them or when they have been unkind or abusive to you?

___ 14. Do you overreact to situations that aren't really a big deal (or do others tell you that you do)?

___ 15. Do you have a pessimistic view of the world or of your future?

___ 16. Do you expect special treatment from people who don't know you?

___ 17. Do you have relationships with individuals who call you "high maintenance" or "needy"?

___ 18. Do you startle at unexpected noises, loud voices, movements, or emotional reactions in others?

___ 19. Do you have difficulty saying "no," or do you say "yes" when you mean "no"?

___ 20. Do you regret decisions you make?

___ 21. Do you dismiss your needs as unimportant or have difficulty even knowing what your needs are?

___ 22. Do you distrust the intentions of people who are nice to you even when they've never given you a reason to doubt them?

___ 23. Do you have trouble committing to relationships, or, if you've made a commitment, do you have trouble honoring it?

___ 24. Do you gloss over (or deny) "red flags" at the beginning of intimate relationships or friendships and then feel betrayed when problems develop later on?

___ 25. Do you feel that problems or "bad" things that happen are your fault even when you know or others tell you they're not?

_____   YOUR TOTAL SCORE

Once you've finished and added up your score, refer to the evaluation below to discover how deeply your wounds continue to keep you heart-sensitive and interrupt your thriving.

Note: If you scored between 0 and 5, any traces of emotional wounds should almost be nonexistent. However, if you feel that some of the symptoms of a sensitive heart are affecting your behavior or beliefs, then you could be in denial regarding a number of areas. In that case, read the evaluations for Levels 1 through 4 to see which one strikes the most responsive chord.

Level One:	6–24 points
Level Two:	25–49 points
Level Three:	50–74 points
Level Four:	75–100 points

If you are a Level One, you suffer a low amount of pain from emotional sensitivities. You may have done some healing work through self-help or therapy, may not have experienced your childhood as wounding, or you may have really done some positive mending in your life to make whatever you experienced less debilitating than it once was or could have been. Or, if you were badly wounded, you may have that wonderful constitution where even the worst events roll off your back, leaving you relatively unscathed. Nevertheless, you can benefit from this book because there is another level of emotional well-being—healthy-heartedness—that you may wish to attain.

If you are a Level Two, you are likely to experience a significant amount of distress in your day-to-day living and in your relationships. While you are probably not a complete prisoner to suffering, you may be, at times, driven by fear and anger rather than by conscious, rational decision-making. By entering a reactive mode, you may end relationships prematurely to avoid possible revictimization.

You're prone to becoming defensive, and you believe the only way to protect yourself from inevitable danger is to cut it off before it even begins to happen. As a matter of fact, you may avoid relationships entirely or only have superficial ones, figuring they will deteriorate anyway. You're likely to perceive more behaviors as wounding and as a bigger deal than they actually are in order to avoid any possibility of further emotional trauma. This style becomes an insurance policy to keep you safe. Yet this over-inclusion of behaviors into the category of wounds reduces your opportunities for spontaneity and for a passionate existence.

You tend to be on the lookout for potential emotional "wounders" in your life. You may unknowingly attract and select individuals who confirm your perception that people can't be trusted. Because of your past fears, you may limit the delight of meeting new people.

If you are a Level Three, you probably wonder why you continue to be unhappy and chronically hurt in your relationships. You may feel like a victim of bad circumstances. If there were a hundred people in a room with ninety-nine of them "nice," you'd be likely to find the one bad apple among them. You probably experience yourself as powerless and have difficulty seeing available choices and options.

You may believe you don't deserve anything better and find yourself stuck between a rock and a hard place. You rationalize wounding behavior from others as something you caused or deserved. Equally disturbing, you may fail to perceive such behavior in others: it's what you're most familiar with, and you don't know to expect anything different. On top of that, you may not recognize or take seriously the possibility that *you* might be wounding others, rationalizing that you have no other choice.

If you are a Level Four, you probably constantly sacrifice your needs for the sake of others. You live in a psychological prison with maximum security, not able to see any escape. Because of intense shame, self-doubt, or self-hatred, you may not be able to accept acts of kindness even when right in front of you. You're so used to being mistreated that you may not know any other kind of treatment exists. You desperately want to feel better, but you may not know where to turn for help. You also may not trust the help that is available. You may have become a walking magnet for mistreatment. Abusive people have radar for spotting you because they are consciously or unconsciously searching for someone to exploit, and you display all the hallmarks of the perfect target.

With all this, you may also be in an emotionally wounding or abusive relationship right now. If so, especially if the abuse is severe, like physical battering, please refer to the Resources section at the back of this book for information to help you get out of immediate danger. This book alone will not be enough. You, too, can become healthy-hearted, but you will need to take more drastic measures in addition to the help offered in this book. The Resources section provides suggestions on where to turn for counseling and/or treatment.

This test gives you an opportunity to see how a sensitive heart can keep you trapped. However, sensitive-hearted people share many specific characteristics, traits, and behaviors that can create problems, pain, and separation. Maybe you didn't relate to the different levels of heart-sensitivity described above. Still, the symptoms detailed in the next chapter might provide a flash of recognition, either about yourself or someone you care for. If so, don't worry. Recognition simply paves the way for the sensitive-hearted to thrive at last.

Chapter Two

Signs of a
Sensitive Heart

The test in the previous chapter gave you a general idea of your level of functioning and of how intensely your sensitive heart has been impacting your life. To help you understand these dynamics more fully, this chapter describes the ten most common signs of a sensitive heart along with examples of how they can appear in daily life.

If you recognize some or many of these characteristics in yourself or in someone you love or care for, don't despair. This may be the first time you've made the link to traumas or unhealed wounds from your childhood. Recognition paves the way for healing your wounds. Facing these tendencies square on puts you on the road to Thriver living.

Once you recognize these attributes, you gain the power to change them. Of course, they once served an important protective function in your childhood. But, since you're going to learn how to prevent further despair, you probably won't have much use for them anymore.

As you read, make a note of each characteristic you identify with. Start thinking of examples from your own life. Later, you'll do an exercise to enable you to focus more specifically on the areas causing you the most upset and interference with your eventual thriving.

THE TOP TEN SYMPTOMS OF
A SENSITIVE HEART

1. Having limited tolerance of differences.
2. Experiencing confusion about control.
3. Being compulsively "nice."
4. Feeling jittery and jumpy.
5. Visualizing tragedy (catastrophic thinking).
6. Expecting special treatment.
7. Personalizing the impersonal.
8. Tending to self-destruction.
9. Having boundary problems.
10. Having intimacy troubles.

1. HAVING LIMITED TOLERANCE
OF DIFFERENCES

People with sensitive hearts often feel threatened when others don't notice what they notice or react the way they react. Any discrepancy in another person's reaction can be intimidating and, at times, incorrectly interpreted as hostile or confrontational.

For instance, if your parents failed to validate or even acknowledge your opinions, feelings, and thoughts, you may have a strong need for others to constantly agree with you or else it activates the old wound of longing for acknowledgment. In a more extreme case, if a woman has been abused—from inappropriate sexual remarks or touch to full-blown molestation—she may become extremely distressed upon seeing explicit material. Likewise, people who were battered physically or verbally may see dramatizations of violence and physically respond as if they, not the characters on the screen, are being beaten.

If you experience some form of limited tolerance, you may become frightened, angry, or judgmental when others do not share your response or if they are concerned about issues like freedom of expression. You may want to ban violent and/or sexual images in the media and demonize people who disagree with you.

You may also underreact. For instance, where most people would be horrified at a grisly murder scene, those with sensitive hearts who've tried to cut off their feelings may be numb. For those especially wounded, observing violence or other disturbing images may be so commonplace that they don't even recognize the images as violent.

You may be extremely sensitive to anything that looks, smells, or remotely resembles previously endured mistreatment. People who have limited tolerance need to understand that others who have not had their experiences often will not respond as they do.

Susie's father frequently erupted into out-of-control rages, throwing things around the house, slamming doors, and occasionally hitting her. Though many of these rages subsided before resulting in a physical lashing-out, Susie could not accurately predict when he would erupt, let alone how severely. She lived in constant fear for her safety.

As an adult, Susie attracted passionate men who often expressed themselves with a raised voice or animated body language. When Carl talked even a little bit louder, Susie reacted as if she were about to be hit, accusing him of abusing her. He hadn't been wounded in the way she was and had never demonstrated violent behavior either before or during their relationship. Her accusations stunned him. He would lower his voice and reassure her he was expressing himself passionately, not abusively. She did not believe she could trust him. She could not understand that others without such a sensitive heart probably would not react to his volume with the same intensity. And, of course, before she began her healing process, she could not acknowledge this discrepancy without thinking that something was wrong with her.

2. EXPERIENCING CONFUSION
ABOUT CONTROL

People with sensitive hearts tend to be confused about control in the sense of what they do and do not have power over. When with a partner who doesn't understand a sensitive heart or with one who adds insult to injury, the wounded partner often resorts to peacemaking behaviors or to obsessively trying to figure out what she did wrong to provoke her partner's negative or irrational behavior. People with sensitive hearts don't understand that another person's irrational behavior has nothing to do with them or that it's nothing they can prevent, stop, or change. Everyone, at times, responds to others in less than ideal ways, such as with irritation, judgment, or criticism. For the heart-sensitive, however, even minor insults can feel like an assault because they trigger feelings of helplessness. People with unhealed wounds don't understand that mistreatment is the responsibility of the one doing the mistreating, not the person receiving it.

Conversely, people with sensitive hearts also often have difficulty correctly identifying areas where they do have control. This makes them likely to stay in unhealthy situations far too long. "Why doesn't she leave him?" many might wonder about a woman whose layers of makeup barely cover her bruises. Unfortunately, the option to walk out, to reject abuse as a way of life, doesn't exist in her consciousness.

In healthy families, children are gradually given more and more choices as they grow. They develop a sense of mastery appropriate to their development. But children who suffered mistreatment within their families or from outside sources, such as being the target of prejudice, racism, or sexism, are powerless. Their developmental needs are disregarded. They develop illusions of control, hoping to change the behavior of others. They carry these illusions into adulthood.

If you suffer this confusion, you must understand that you'll never "fix" those who mistreat you (your family, friends, people in the workplace, or society at large). You can certainly influence change through proactive methods, but no one can ever *make* anyone else change. To accept that you cannot change others is to give up inappropriate hope. For a sensitive heart, this can seem devastating or unbearably disappointing, but it is absolutely necessary for full healing and for eventual thriving.

3. BEING COMPULSIVELY "NICE"

Adam, whose father ridiculed him for every mistake, constantly apologized for himself, even when he did nothing wrong. Remember Susan, who learned to be a meticulous housekeeper to ward off her mother's criticism? After her marriage to Bob, she continued to compulsively clean. She convinced herself that this was what a "nice" wife provides for her husband. She dreaded that her husband would be angry if her efforts at cleanliness lapsed even a little.

On the more extreme end, Candace, a victim of severe sexual and physical abuse, is so terrified of being hurt again that she cannot let even a stranger pass by without waving, smiling, or saying hello. She fears the aggression that might result if she doesn't make some placating gesture.

People with sensitive hearts crave being liked and getting approval. It's their reassurance that they won't be hurt again. So they tend to be excessively nice, even to those with whom they have only a tenuous connection, only determining their own needs in relation to others. Underneath all of this is an obsession with warding off pain and maintaining safety from further injury.

I don't want to imply that there is anything wrong with courtesy and respect. It's a question of motivation. People with unhealed wounds frequently come from fear and a diminished sense of self. There is often something unreal about their "niceness." In reality, they remain virtual prisoners of other people's opinions. They cannot choose the way they want to be.

4. FEELING JITTERY AND JUMPY

The adrenaline rush we get when we're afraid is nature's gift when we are normal and healthy. It helps us identify real danger and gives us the burst of energy we need to either run away or fight. But the fears of people with sensitive hearts are often based on imagined dangers. They are remnants of childhood fear that was ignored, denied, or that wasn't permissible to express. When fears are not appropriately resolved, they get displaced onto normally benign occurrences.

At Levels Three and Four, someone may jump at a ringing phone or a knock on the door. In some extreme cases of verbal or physical abuse, even animated conversation may be upsetting. Sometimes the "link" to the childhood mistreatment will be obvious, such as "My mother became enraged while talking on the phone and took it out on me." Other responses may need further investigation. No matter what, people with sensitive hearts believe they need these reactions to protect themselves from the possibility of further mistreatment.

Jennifer, a thirty-year-old woman whose mother often yelled at her, grew up to be unusually agitated, especially around loud noises. To Jennifer, the shouting was injurious to her emotional well-being. Jennifer grew up on constant alert, listening for cues that her mother would become angry and shout at her. She adapted by learning ways to manipulate her mother into calming down.

If she hadn't overcompensated by being so alert, she believed her mother's reprimands might have been more frequent or more severe. In her childhood predicament, as you can see, Jennifer's jumpiness served to protect her. But as an adult, it kept her in a state of chronic stress and interfered with her capacity to work.

5. VISUALIZING TRAGEDY (CATASTROPHIC THINKING)

People with sensitive hearts frequently experience images of impending doom, often projecting the worst in all situations. Those of my clients who endured abuse sometimes report flashes of death scenes even when they are not in dangerous situations. Experiences like walking under a freeway bridge, driving a car, or even a time of day, like twilight, may stir visions of annihilation. Once again, there is usually a "link" to childhood violence or neglect.

> *It makes sense that people repeatedly exposed to danger in the forms of mistreatment or neglect will be vigilant about the possibilities of danger, even when no dangerous stimuli are present. Coupled with excessive vigilance is the belief that "bad" things are inevitably going to happen. Once again, there is the illusion that it would be possible to stave off impending catastrophe if only one could "figure out" the predictors. These people often find it very difficult to focus on the positive, the potential for good, or on opportunities for success. They often overgeneralize behavior as mistreatment that others who don't suffer a sensitive heart might categorize as only moderately annoying or even fairly benign.*

Paradoxically, the individual's focus on the negative can bring on a disastrous result, simply through the expectation of catastrophe. Remember Tom? His mother threatened to send him to boarding school whenever he failed to follow her instructions. Of course, she certainly had a right to impose a consequence for what she deemed as inappropriate behavior, like adding a chore to his weekly routine. But threatening to send him away only terrified him! While he would become more compliant to appease her, he did so out of fear, not out of genuine learning.

As an adult, Tom frequently imagined the worst in many situations. He chronically feared his girlfriend was going to break up with him if he ever disappointed or upset her. He could not imagine that she had any room for his imperfections. He actually drew comfort from expecting her to leave him because this allowed him to feel more ready for this disaster if it were to actually happen. After several years of repeatedly accusing his girlfriend of planning to end the relationship, she got sick and tired of endlessly reassuring him. She ended their relationship.

To thrive, you must learn to distinguish situations that are actually harmful in the present from those that appear harmful because they are viewed solely through the lens of a wounded child. You must learn to make room for positive outcomes and a hopeful future.

6. EXPECTING SPECIAL TREATMENT

People with sensitive hearts who have done some healing and have become aware of the degree of their deprivation may go through a phase of demanding that the world cater to their sensitivities and needs. They may expect lovers or spouses to be perfect mind readers, to anticipate their fears and cravings, or to be responsible for their happiness, creativity, and spiritual well-being. They may wish others to forego their own needs and focus primarily on them. Essentially, they want compensation for all their years of emotional starvation. Understandably, they often don't know what's reasonable to ask for or how to ask. For some, there is a conscious acknowledgment of this desire for special treatment, but for most, the expectation operates unconsciously.

Remember John, who became enraged whenever he had to stand in line, even for events he looked forward to attending? Even visits to the bank, the movies, or the supermarket held the potential for high drama. He desperately wanted immediate gratification because of how long he had been required to wait as a child to get any of his needs met. As an adult, John believed his demands were reasonable. But the world repeatedly disappointed him. Paradoxically, he had expectations far too low in his significant relationships. He needed to learn to expect more from the people with whom he shared intimacy and less from the impersonal world.

Margaret's parents generally provided a loving and supportive environment. However, because they struggled financially and suffered embarrassment about not being able to give their children much more than the bare necessities, they had a hard time allowing Margaret to express disappointment when she didn't get the things she wanted. They could not accept their financial situation. Margaret's disappointment evoked humiliation in them. To avoid shame, they told Margaret that she was selfish for wanting things she knew they could not afford. They were well meaning, but they unfortunately taught Margaret to suppress her dreams and desires. She feared that she would lose her parents' approval if she openly expressed them.

In adulthood, Margaret unknowingly expected others to grant her special favors. When she was short on money, she believed that if her friends really cared about her, they would pay her way when they went out for dinner, to the movies, bowling, and so on. She perceived herself as the disadvantaged one, even though many of her friends also struggled to make ends meet.

Very often, instead of expressing desires and concerns directly, the people with sensitive hearts act out with sulks, rages, emotional withdrawal, or even infidelity or theft. They very often have no idea of how to distinguish between appropriate and inappropriate demands.

7. PERSONALIZING THE IMPERSONAL

People with unhealed wounds are notorious for claiming personal responsibility for things, events, moods, and emotions that have nothing to do with them or they may believe that others are out to get them.

Melody was convinced that the traffic was worse when she got on the road, that she was jinxed, that other drivers set out to make her commute particularly miserable. It never occurred to Melody that her work hours dictated that she drive during rush hour, that the carelessness of other drivers was not specifically aimed at her, or that there were indeed other drivers as thoughtful as she was.

One night, a close friend invited Angela to a party. Angela did not know the host but agreed to go. During the party, Angela overheard the host tell another guest who wanted more potato chips that he had run out. The guest didn't seem particularly bothered, nor did the host seem to feel remorseful about running out of chips, especially since there were plenty of other things to munch on. Angela, however, because of her tendency to personalize the impersonal, automatically assumed that the guests would be unhappy and that the host would feel bad for not having enough chips.

Even though Angela could in no way rationally be held accountable for the absence of chips, she jumped in without even thinking and offered to go out and buy more. Of course, she really didn't want to run to the store. But since she couldn't bear the thought of anyone being disappointed, she took it upon herself to prevent that possibility. Angela's childhood experiences left her with the belief that, if others get disappointed or upset, they will make it her fault. So, of course, she worked overtime to keep others from experiencing disappointment.

If you personalize to this extent, you may experience the world as hostile, blaming, and unforgiving. You probably take too few opportunities to relax and just take care of your own business. Most of the time you're too busy figuring out who is angry, disappointed, or unhappy with you and speculating about what you've done wrong.

8. TENDING TO SELF-DESTRUCTION

People with sensitive hearts often have no sense of how to take care of themselves. They often treat their bodies unkindly. Some use drugs or alcohol to excess. Some go days without eating. Others may eat at any sign of distress, even when they're not hungry. These individuals seldom know how to read their bodies' cues. They sleep too much or not enough. They may isolate themselves for days without any consideration for the basic human need for contact. Or, they may perpetually engage with other people, never recognizing their need for solitude and sepa- rateness from others. Some are even unaware of personal hygiene.

They often unconsciously put themselves in dangerous situ- ations. Because they don't pay adequate attention to their safety, they are more likely to be targets of other's exploitations or even for violent crimes. This is not their fault, of course. But, had they cared more about themselves to begin with, they would have made different choices about where to be. One young woman, Elaine, had been date raped on several occa- sions. While she held no responsibility for the actual rapes, she eventually realized that her choices were reflective of someone who didn't care much about herself.

On one occasion, Elaine went home with a guy she'd met in a bar after several drinks. He promised her they would just watch a movie together. She believed him, in spite of having no data about his trustworthiness. I'm sure you can figure out the rest.

Once Elaine came to value herself, she no longer placed herself in potentially dangerous situations. She

25

neither hurt her own body nor allowed others such easy ability to hurt her.

9. HAVING BOUNDARY PROBLEMS

Boundaries are the distinction between you and other people or between you and the outside world. Violence, sexual abuse, and even verbal harassment blur that distinction. So do neglect, abandonment, and emotional distance. In fact, any experience where a child's *essential* needs are frustrated or denied can result in boundary problems. Those with sensitive hearts have difficulty knowing intuitively what's right for their bodies, minds, and spirits. They may tolerate too much, then abruptly say "no." Their messages about closeness and distance are confusing to others. When it comes to starting, continuing, or ending relationships, their judgment may be skewed.

For example, Veronica, who received excessive attention for her physical attractions, was relatively unnoticed for all her wonderful inner qualities. She didn't grow to experience that her body belonged to her. As an adult, she unknowingly re-created her wound by becoming highly provocative and flirtatious with men who were strangers. She would draw them in, then suddenly feel overwhelmed and invaded. She had no early warning signal that would tell her when to gracefully ask for space or distance. She could only overreact, surprising and possibly hurting the other person. What she really wanted was attention for her inner self, but she had no idea how to attract it.

10. HAVING INTIMACY TROUBLES

There is, today, an epidemic of dysfunction in intimate relationships. People with unhealed hearts, however, experience difficulties in love more painfully than do those who either weren't wounded or haven't re-created the wounding process in their adult lives. Typical problems may include:

- Difficulty trusting your partner.
- Keeping your options open for escape (one foot in the door, one foot out), watching the exits.
- Examining your partner's flaws under a microscope, convinced that they will blossom into mistreatment or neglect of you.
- Difficulty trusting your own judgment and perceptions.
- Terror of abandonment (especially if the partner requests space).
- Constantly taking the temperature of the relationship.
- Tendency to create drama or conflict; not trusting harmony.
- Not wanting to be pitied for past suffering, but desperately needing compassion; frequently confusing the two.
- Acting like everything is okay, fearing the consequences of speaking up, fearing being perceived as a burden.
- Concerns about being perceived as "damaged goods."
- Being overwhelmed by neutral or mildly provocative stimuli.
- Tendency to project malicious intent onto benevolent partners.
- Glossing over (or denying) red flags at the beginning of relationships, then feeling betrayed when problems develop.
- Choosing hurtful partners and then re-creating the atmosphere of childhood wounds, feeling trapped and unable to leave.

TAKING THE FIRST STEP TOWARD HEALING

Now that you've read through the ten common symptoms, which ones do you identify with? To enhance your recognition, go back through the list and highlight the ones that describe you. Then write out the symptom with as many examples as you can think of from your own life that illustrate how the symptom manifests. Do this for each of the symptoms you relate to. The more thorough you are, the more benefits you'll reap. Also, if you notice additional symptoms or characteristics that you believe interfere with your living fully, feel free to list and describe them along with those I've listed. Remember, change is only possible when there is awareness and acceptance of what is.

I encourage you to really give this some thought. It's not easy doing such intensive self-examination, especially if this is your first time recognizing any of these attributes and connecting them to your sensitive heart. Even for those of you who have already gone through other methods of self-help or therapy, it often remains difficult to honestly assess your own process and can even be quite overwhelming at times.

I hope these descriptions offer you some comfort in recognizing that you are not alone. However, if you are embarrassed by what you discover, I encourage you to practice compassion. Nurture yourself. To thrive, you need to put down the hammer and stop beating yourself on the head. There is nothing wrong with you for having developed these qualities. They are normal responses to abnormal events. You need to respect and value how they have served you. Do not look upon these qualities with disdain or contempt. These attributes constituted an effective and adaptive language for your childhood. Now it's time to learn a new one that fits adulthood where you have the power and the choice to no longer feel or be wounded.

Chapter Three

How Did Your Heart Become Sensitive?

Most people, if not all, had a childhood experience that left an emotional scar. For most, the wounds were probably fairly mild, nothing that created too much fallout or heart sensitivity. Or, if the wounds were more severe, there was also plenty of positive stuff to counterbalance the impact of the wounds so the scars could quickly fade and become insignificant. For many children, however, the wounds were deep or the impact more profound, and the scars have never faded. It also happens that a particular child can be more vulnerable than other children and more likely to feel wounds more intensely. In all cases, if the wounds remain unhealed, the consequences continue to impact our lives throughout adulthood by leaving a bruised or sensitive heart.

As children, we are extremely vulnerable to emotional wounds, regardless of whether they are inflicted intentionally. Because of the dependent nature of children, early wounds leave us vulnerable to believing that we deserve them. The belief that we are responsible for mistreatment or unfortunate circumstances adds an additional layer of sensitivity. But no child ever deserves to be treated badly or neglected, period.

Children do not have the same choices as adults. If wrong was done to you or you were subjected to circumstances you weren't developmentally ready for, it's critical that you do not blame yourself. So as you go through the process of uncovering how you became sensitive-hearted, please try not to judge whether you have a right to feel wounded about something, even something you think others would call trivial. All that matters for the purpose of healing is that you feel you were mistreated or deprived of something essential. If that's true, you have unhealed wounds that need attention. Healing doesn't even require you to recall all the details of how you were hurt. But it does require you to honestly admit to the things that remain unfinished and that continue to hurt you. You must first accept the presence of your wounds and their resulting sensitivities in order to heal them.

The categories that follow describe a broad range of possible ways you may have been wounded and might hence have developed a sensitive heart. While I've tried to include many possible examples, please understand that I may have missed some. Since it's such a subjective experience, it would be impossible to address every conceivable situation that might hurt a child.

If you feel you were wounded by something I didn't address, don't rule out your wound as unimportant. Again, what matters is how you feel about your experiences. If you planned to take someone to court for past abuse, corroboration of your account would be critical. For the purpose of psychological healing, our purpose, objective definitions of mistreatment don't matter.

As you read through all the variations of how you might have been wounded, you may discover that things you thought weren't so bad were actually worse than you thought while other things were not so bad after all. You may have experienced things listed under "abuse" without feeling wounded by them. Many factors determine whether a situation is wounding, such as your age at the time, the level of positive influence surrounding negative experiences, your temperament, the way you processed the negative situation, and so on. If such experiences truly didn't bother you, there's no need to make something out of nothing. While some injuries may be considered more universally wounding, the process is really quite subjective and individual. It's common for two people who've experienced the same situation to have entirely different reactions. So please, begin your healing process by reading with an open mind and open heart. As I will remind you throughout this book, change can only occur with the acceptance of what is.

HOW WE BECOME HEART-SENSITIVE

Heart sensitivity comes from unhealed emotional wounds. Emotional wounds come in many different forms and from many different places. They may come through words or actions. They may be intentionally or unintentionally inflicted. Although people have traditionally looked to the parents to understand how children become wounded, I want to quickly destroy this premise. While parents can be the source of injury, wounds can just as easily come from siblings, teachers, peers, society, or any other influential person or institution in a child's life. They may come from the neighborhood bully or a frightening stranger in the park. Wounds also vary in intensity and impact. The same innocuous, offhand remark might be devastating to one child but only mildly upsetting to another.

As you can see, it's not an easy task to define "wounding behavior." Sometimes it's blatant enough to force agreement. Take Holly, for example. Holly was forced to have sex with her grandfather, father, and brother, starting from the age of ten. When Holly told her mother what was happening, her mother told her she was "crazy" and that if she didn't stop spreading rumors, she would be sent away. I can't imagine anyone not thinking that this poor child was abused.

Remember Philip? His mother was depressed and self-absorbed. She would yell at him whenever frustration got the best of her. When she was in a positive state of mind, she would also hug him and say how much she loved him. Was he wounded? Compare him to Craig, a child in another home. His father had a pretty volatile temper, but Craig was the kind of kid who wasn't bothered by loud voices. Whereas Philip harbored deep pain from the times his mother raged at him, Craig remained unscathed.

The legal system only recognizes severe forms of abuse as damaging to children (physical, sexual, abandonment, or neglect). But so many other things can scar our hearts. For instance, no court would prosecute a parent for calling a child "stupid." But the behavior can still cause emotional damage. While I in no way want to trivialize the subject of child abuse, I do want to give you permission to fully embrace your wounds without getting caught up in objective, legal definitions of mis-treatment or abuse.

Because such a massive range of behaviors and experiences can wound a child, categorization becomes quite challenging. For the sake of simplicity, I've used the following distinctions: dysfunction, abuse (physical, sexual, or psychological), and neglect/abandonment. I've also included a brief section on cul-tural/societal insults, like racism and prejudice; social portrayals and images can have a profound effect on our development, even when family life was pretty good. For each category, I've included some examples. Again, please note that while primary caregivers usually have the most influence and potential for wounding a child, wounds may also come from other relatives or caregivers, peers, siblings, teachers, coaches, and so on.

The bad news is that anyone with a meaningful role in your childhood had the power to hurt you and affect how you grew to feel about yourself. But there's good news, too. You can heal from the hurt, turn your scars into resources and treasures, and learn to prevent further insult. (We'll talk more about that later.)

Keep in mind that while intentions certainly matter to adults, when it comes to children, a wound is a wound is a wound. Some of your wounds may be the consequence of things completely outside of anyone's control. Those things still hurt you emotionally, and they still require healing. If someone were to accidentally break your arm by smashing it in a door, the fact of the accident wouldn't make your arm hurt or need medical attention any less. Emotional wounds are similar. They hurt regardless of whether they were purposefully, accidentally, or unconsciously inflicted. So don't let your mind rationalize someone else's hurtful behavior just because they didn't mean to hurt you. Intentions only matter to adults. Children don't know the difference; they only feel the hurt.

DYSFUNCTION

Everyone's childhood was dysfunctional to some degree. While all forms of abuse constitute dysfunction, all dysfunction is not abusive.

In dysfunctional families with no abuse, caregivers usually have good intentions. They do not commit major boundary violations, and generally they will own up to their mistakes when their children express feelings of hurt or show signs of being wounded. They don't intentionally shame or humiliate their children. They don't blame their children for errors in their own judgment. They have some empathy. Usually, children of dysfunctional families enter adulthood without the added burden of feeling responsible for their caregivers' mistakes. But dysfunctional behavior can also wreak havoc on a child's emotional and psychological development, especially if the dysfunction is chronic and pervasive.

Take Leslie, for example. Leslie's mother, Karen, was crippled in a car accident when Leslie was only eight. Karen's identity and self-worth had been largely based on being a good mom. After the accident, she felt useless and ashamed that she could no longer carry out her usual motherly activities. Karen was never offered counseling. She grew up in a family that considered seeking help from people outside one's family taboo.

Because no one wanted her to feel any worse than she already felt, the family sheltered her from her despair and shame.

Leslie was the youngest and most sensitive of the three children. She felt alone in her own suffering and wanted desperately to talk about her feelings. But because of the unspoken family code not to upset mom, she lived with her unhappiness in silence. She didn't want to be a burden. For the most part, her mother and father were loving and provided the best they could under the circumstances. But they were so preoccupied with protecting mom that they failed to recognize Leslie's suffering.

This scenario clearly illustrates an unfortunate situation in which no one is to blame. The family lived under difficult circumstances. Many of you reading this might think that Leslie had no right to feel cheated or hurt by what happened to her. But Leslie did suffer. She realized just how much she had suffered once she noticed as an adult that she continually attracted men who ignored her feelings.

Another very common form of dysfunction happens when parents who were mistreated as children make a conscious decision never to mistreat their own children. In doing so, they go to the other extreme of permissiveness and indulgence. It is difficult for a child growing up in this kind of environment to recognize that she is being wounded emotionally. A too-permissive environment hinders the child from developing a tolerance to frustration (the impossibility of having everything she wants) and the ability to control her impulses. This developmental deprivation may not become apparent until adulthood. Jim's mother, for example, "loved" him so much that she never wanted to say "no" to him. As an adult, he would become completely enraged if his girlfriend didn't want to do what he wanted. And since his mom never taught him self-reliance, he never learned how to care for himself. She needed him to stay dependent on her so she could continue to show her love by constantly doing things for him. Clearly, she had the best intentions. She did not want her son to experience the pain she had suffered. Inadvertently, she ended up creating an entirely different kind of pain.

ABUSE

Child abuse is mistreatment to a child's core being. It is perpetrated by those responsible for the child's development. Abuse may include physical battering, sexual abuse, verbal abuse, loud yelling, name-calling (such as "dummy," "you dog," or constant diminishment), abandonment, and/or neglect. This mistreatment is consistent, and it persists throughout childhood. It indicates an attitude of chronic disrespect for the child's developmental needs. Abusers frequently feel entitled to their behavior. Their rationalizations include beliefs like the following:

"It's my child."
"It's for his own good."
"It's to teach her a lesson."
"He deserves it!"

Many times the abusive caregiver perceives her intent as benevolent. Often, even when shown or told that their behavior is damaging, abusers disregard the input and don't change. Patsy's mother beat her with objects to teach her a lesson. The mother actually believed that her methods were her only way to teach essential lessons in proper behavior. She believed she was disciplining her child effectively and would have been appalled at the attribution of abuse. She believed the old adage "Spare the rod, spoil the child." She did not want to spoil her child.

Abuse violates the rights of the child. Abusive behavior would be criminal if perpetrated by one unrelated adult upon another (and would be termed battery, assault, rape, etc.). Abusers are characterized by a profound sense of victimization, coupled with a sense of entitlement to do what they are doing. They lack empathy. Because children need their parents' care, they have no choice but to buy the message they deserve abuse.

In cases where abuse to a child comes from outside the family, the wounds can be just as devastating. In this case, the family's response can either minimize or exacerbate the impact. Eleanor was repeatedly touched inappropriately by a friend's father, who threatened to harm her family if she told. When Eleanor told her mother, she confronted the man and removed her daughter from the relationship. The molestation left Eleanor with significant trust issues, but at least she escaped further injury because her mother responded lovingly and appropriately.

Lisa, on the other hand, suffered a double injury. As a teenager, she was raped while out partying. She did not tell anyone about the rape because she was supposed to be studying with a friend. She feared the consequences of having lied to her parents. She kept the trauma a secret and lived for years with the unresolved issues. In this case, while the parents were not to blame for the actual rape, they still bear some culpability. Lisa couldn't trust that her parents' concern for her well-being would supercede their anger at the lie.

Jill was molested by a babysitter. The actual molestation was not as deeply scarring as the fact that her mother knew the man's proclivities and hired him anyway. When the daughter reported the abuse to her mother, the mother called her daughter "crazy" and accused her of inventing the story. Her mother's betrayal was the most difficult thing for Jill to resolve.

PHYSICAL ABUSE

Have you ever tried to have a rational conversation with a two-year-old in a parking lot or on a street corner? You know that an occasional physical intervention may be warranted, like a smack on the bottom or the simple need to pick up the child and place her back on the curb. Some may argue that these methods reflect even more effective parenting than a discussion the child is not developmentally ready for. Most parents also occasionally "lose it" and yell or scream in the stress of the moment. But whether these moments produce lasting scars depends largely on whether the parent acknowledges her mistake and keeps from blaming or ridiculing a child for a hurt reaction.

Even the threat of physical violence intimidates a child and threatens his sense of safety. Peter's mother never actually raised a hand to him, but if she didn't like his behavior, she would say, "You better stop that or I'll smack you so hard you won't be able to sit for a week."

Sometimes even seemingly playful physical contact like tickling, roughhousing, or wrestling can become violating and potentially damaging if the child's right to say no is ignored or negated. Children love to play and usually enjoy physical contact with their loved ones. But imagine this scenario. A father is playing with his five-year-old son. The boy is laughing in delight, but at some point the tickling becomes uncomfortable or excessive and the boy asks his father to stop. Dad becomes angry. He yells, "You're the one who wanted tickling. Sissy! I'll never play with you again!" This heaps blame and humiliation on the child. It is profoundly disrespectful. We can all get carried away in play. What's important is recognizing children's rights to assert when they've had enough. Children own their own bodies.

SEXUAL ABUSE

In our permissive age, sexual abuse is particularly hard to define. While it's technically against the law for children under eighteen to have sexual intercourse with anyone, including their peers, many are sexually active long before they reach the age of consent. Sex between parents and children has been taboo in most cultures, yet it has also been pervasive throughout history, even modern history. When accompanied by physical force, of course, such sexual relationships are abusive. But what about sex that appears voluntary? What about sexual intercourse that the child claims to have enjoyed or benefited from? What about fondling or lewd comments? What about the way society sexually objectifies women and teenage girls in the media? Do these constitute abuse?

What about a grandfather who has a moment of poor impulse control and grabs at his fourteen-year-old granddaughter's newly emerging breasts? Some might say this was just a one-time slip. But does that make it any less abusive or emotionally damaging? And what if the daughter can't trust her parents to put a stop to such behavior? Most likely, she will suffer severe betrayal and have critical boundary and trust issues for years to come.

On the other hand, what about sex between a seventeen-year-old and a twenty-two-year-old who have been dating for a year? Is this abuse? Some would say "yes" and others "no." Of course if coercion existed, then the answer would be "yes." Also, it might be that for a mature seventeen-year-old there would be no repercussions. But to a less mature child or one who possibly had other emotional wounds, this act could be devastating—even if voluntary—especially if the partner had promised love but turned out to be in it just for the sex.

Difference in power is the main criteria used to determine whether a situation is abusive. Strength, size, status, and need for care are the factors that determine power relationships. Cynthia's brother repeatedly harassed her when she was twelve and he was fifteen. He showed her pornographic pictures to express his desires. He threatened her with violence if she refused to comply. Since other adult relatives were also abusing her, she had no one to turn to for help. She was truly powerless.

In contrast, a fifteen-year-old girl whose ten-year-old brother approached her for sex play might not perceive her situation as abusive if she could tell her parents without shame and if they were willing to correct the boy's behavior. If, however, they told her to "handle the situation herself," the parents would be disrespecting the developmental needs of both children.

The bottom line is that any sexual relationship with an adult is damaging to a child's development, even in the form of verbal harassment. It robs a child of rightful innocence. Sometimes incest is gentle, seductive, and accompanied by gifts and special attention. Those violated may rationalize that they have chosen, enjoyed, or benefited from the special attention. Sometimes the abuse is delivered in such subtle ways many people wouldn't even recognize it as abuse.

Whether overt or subtle, seduced children frequently become adults with serious intimacy issues. Many suffer problems with sexual communication, body image, and emotional bonding. They may become impotent, manifest self-destructive or sexually reckless behavior, have difficulty reaching orgasm, or be entirely turned off to any form of sexual behavior. They may confuse sexual desire and lust with love. They may unknowingly seek out relationships with people who mistreat them physically.

Betsi's cousin touched her inappropriately when she was fourteen. When she became sexually active in her late teens, she went for guys who only wanted sex. She longed for love and kindness, but since her body had been mistreated, she did not know how to distinguish someone who was genuinely interested in her from someone who was just using her sexually. She was constantly disappointed. Eventually, she grew to dislike and distrust men.

PSYCHOLOGICAL/EMOTIONAL ABUSE

There are as many varieties of psychological mistreatment as there are cereals on the market shelves. Here, too, what might be inconsequential behavior for one child might be devastating to another. Some of the most potentially wounding forms of psychological abuse include name-calling, threatening of abandonment, deprivation or physical violence, intentional humiliation, shame or ridicule, blame, and/or devaluing a child's expressed interests, needs, and opinions.

Ben's father was so filled with shame that he couldn't acknowledge his mistakes. In order to avoid feeling bad about himself, he constantly put Ben down. One time, Ben didn't do one of his assigned chores; he forgot to take out the trash. His dad, who repeatedly failed to follow through on his responsibilities, saw this as the opportune moment to degrade his son. Rather than look at his own limitations and accept responsibility for them, he said to his son, "No wonder I can't get anything done around here. You're so spoiled, I have to spend all my time getting on you." He did not teach his son about responsibility. He blamed and degraded him.

NEGLECT AND ABANDONMENT

When a child is repeatedly left unattended or is threatened with abandonment or emotional withdrawal, the child becomes terrified. Together, the purposeful infliction of deprivation and the resulting terror rob a child of his right to be cared for.

Children are incapable of fulfilling their own emotional, mental, and physical needs. The younger they are, the more dependent they are on parental care. Parents or other significant caregivers must adequately provide for children's basic needs until they are ready for independence. Otherwise, development is stunted and the child's proper growth is endangered. Injury and even death are possible consequences of neglect.

It is not neglectful to explain to a three-year-old, "Mommy will not listen to you if you keep hitting to get your way," and then follow through by not responding until the hitting stops. However, when a child is in distress, it is neglectful to withhold food, love, comfort, or any other basic supply.

A subtle but common form of neglect occurs when an unhappily married parent unconsciously uses a child as a surrogate spouse. Sandy's father often turned to Sandy for emotional comfort when he and Sandy's mother quarreled. She became his confidant. He took her on business trips to keep him company. Of course, he presented those trips as a great opportunity for travel and adventure. However, by the time she was a teenager and starting to date, it became clear that his seemingly altruistic offerings were in service of his emotional needs, not for her development. Under the guise of protecting her, he criticized every guy she liked.

A parent who is unconscious of her own childhood wounds may use a child as a surrogate mother or father. In this case, the parent makes demands of her child that would be appropriate to place on another adult but that are quite inappropriate to expect from a child. In Todd's case, his mother had been emotionally neglected by her father. She had longed for physical affection as a child but never received it. As Todd matured, she became increasingly smothering and had great difficulty respecting his need for independence and separateness.

Our emotional needs as children are enormous, as well they should be. We are dependent on others for everything until maturation and positive environmental stimuli ready us for independence. Below is a list of our inherent needs. Look at it closely. Did you receive an adequate fulfillment of each when you were a kid?

- Need for closeness and separateness.
- Need for loving physical touch.
- Need for attention, praise, and acknowledgment.
- Need for comfort, nurturing, and reassurance of personal value and specialness.
- Need for challenge and growth experiences.
- Need to be loved and appreciated for both strengths and limitations.

CULTURAL/SOCIETAL INSULTS

Cultural prejudice, racism, sexism, and media stereotyping can cause and inflame emotional wounds. "Unless you've felt it, you don't get it." That's what I often tell people who say that oppressed or exploited groups have nothing to complain about, that they have the same opportunities as everyone else.

Even those who "should know better" often perpetuate the problem. I am a perfect example. Though I pride myself on having overcome gender stereotyping, and despite the years I have been aware of this problem, I still catch myself slipping into sexist thinking. I will presume that someone's doctor is male and someone's nurse is female. This may seem like no big deal. But if someone has been repeatedly prejudged, such presumptions can be very offensive. These attitudes and beliefs so often pervade our thinking that we frequently don't even recognize them as potentially abusive.

While the quality of parental care you received as a child probably has the most impact on your psychological development (aside from temperament and biological influences), cultural beliefs and their portrayal in the media can also be deeply influential.

For instance, Samantha's profoundly negative body image developed at least in part from the media's emphasis on thinness. Her peer group was obsessed with dieting and physical appeal. Believing she was fat and unattractive, Samantha constantly degraded her body, even though her parents told her time and time again that they loved her. Despite her parent's emotional support, Samantha's negative body image intensified as she dated guys who were completely caught up in these unrealistic standards and who criticized her body. Samantha, like many other young women with eating disorders or body image problems, was wounded by a cultural standard that overemphasized an unrealistic body ideal and by exploitation in the media.

Men can experience similar societal scarring. Joe started therapy at the age of thirty. As a teenager, he endured school-yard bullying and ridicule from a group of older, bigger boys. When he finally told his dad about it, he hoped for a nurturing response. Instead, his dad told him to "stop acting like a wimp; go back and fight." His father thought he was turning his son into a man. But Joe, a nonviolent, sensitive guy, felt completely abandoned by his dad. He had been doubly victimized.

IF YOU LOVE SOMEONE WITH A SENSITIVE HEART

This book can also benefit anyone in a significant relationship with someone whose heart has become especially sensitive. If there is one place where unresolved wounds will surface, it is in the context of intimate relationships.

For adults with unhealed wounds who are on the road to thriving relationships, it is especially nourishing when loved ones truly understand their experience. Those with sensitive hearts often live alone with their memories, bad dreams, and dysfunctional behaviors. They fear that others won't understand their pain. They worry that others may think they are making a mountain out of a molehill. To feel that another person truly believes them and "gets it" is enormously encouraging and actually speeds healing.

If your loved one suffers from a sensitive heart, take the time to lend your much-needed support. Offer a listening ear. Refrain from passing judgment. Get curious, and ask questions to help you understand. Most importantly, stay loving and gentle. If you have difficulty offering such consistency, make sure you get the support you need to keep yourself grounded. You might even consider practicing some of the exercises and suggestions in this book for yourself, as well.

Chapter Four

Breaking Free

You've identified the ways in which your heart may have become sensitive. Now it's time to examine how you have become your own worst enemy, in other words, how you "revictimize" yourself. If you tend to minimize your wounds or if you pile shame on yourself, you cannot begin this investigation without a little preparation. Give yourself a break. Give yourself credit for your injuries, and instead of blaming yourself, try really hard to support yourself instead.

There's nothing wrong with you for having issues to address. We all have them, even people who would like you to believe that they have everything neatly and comfortably in order. You'll learn later how to let go of unnecessary guards against pain and shame, but for now, try to put them on hold.

You simply cannot set yourself free to celebrate life until you recognize how you create your own roadblocks to fully living and loving yourself and others. You need to recognize how the fallout from your emotional scars has directed your behavior. In doing so, you will free yourself from your self-protective shields and the false sense of safety they provide. This freedom makes you ready to thrive and ultimately have the kinds of relationships you long for—those filled with love, kindness, and respect. Otherwise you'll be entrenched in either "bruised" or "sensitive-heart mentality" and limited to less than the joyful life experiences you deserve.

Before we investigate the process of revictimization, let's detour for a moment for a fuller description of "bruised" and "sensitive-heart" mentalities and how they differ from that of a "thriving healthy-heart."

BRUISED-HEART MENTALITY

Bruised-heart mentality reflects an attitude of powerlessness and the absence of choice. Since children are dependent on adults for all survival and developmental needs, children who are treated poorly may be more resigned to a life of suffering. They won't expect anything better. Their hearts become bruised. As life unfolds, the pressures continue to exacerbate the pain.

Child victims, especially the severely abused, rarely have their experiences validated. No one has said to them, "Yes, I've hurt you, and I'm sorry." That's because when people hurt others, they often become defensive to avoid feeling guilty or ashamed. They tend to characterize the abuse as being the fault of the victim.

Others simply believe they have the right to their abusive or harmful behavior. They lack any empathy. Even when a wounded child has been fortunate enough to receive validation and acknowledgment from the wounding source, emotional wounds require a healing process that most people are ill equipped to provide. Thus, the wound remains actively open and sore.

Those with badly bruised hearts tend to believe that they cause everything bad or that only bad things will happen to them. Conversely, anything good that happens occurs only by chance. They view the world through pessimistic lenses. They re-create the patterns of their original wounds in personal, social, and work settings. In essence, they haven't grasped that as adults in big bodies, they now have the power and choice to walk away from unwanted pain.

They frequently feel trapped, hopeless, despairing, and ashamed. Yet even while they're busy taking responsibility for what doesn't belong to them, they often have trouble taking responsibility for the situations they've actually caused. The stance of the bruised heart is passive. It says, "The world has an impact on me, but I have no impact on the world."

Those with bruised hearts often shrink to keep from taking up too much space. Their breathing may actually be shallow, as if they felt guilty for breathing, for being alive, for burdening the world with their presence. They tend to be overwhelmed with grief and self-pity. Or they may be caught in the cycle of desperately needing compassion and understanding from others for their pain yet being unable to accept it when it comes along.

They may provoke intense emotional responses in others. People either want to take care of them or to push them into a happier life. Other people know the victim deserves better, but the victim doesn't. People who love those with bruised-heart mentality often become frustrated and angry at the wounded. They want to help, but the wounded won't allow it.

For those with bruised hearts, this cycle unfortunately reinforces their conviction that they cannot have the kind of unconditional love they deserved and needed in childhood. This may translate to a sense that they are inherently unlovable and undeserving of happiness.

Bruised-heart mentality lies at the extreme left end of the continuum of the sensitive heart. Most people carrying leftover pain from childhood do not live in the world as a total victim. Most have created functional behaviors and beliefs that help them go through life with at least some hope for a better tomorrow. They've become survivors with sensitive hearts and may even exhibit some Thriver traits.

SENSITIVE-HEART MENTALITY

While most people don't realize that childhood wounds can be seriously damaging, we should all remember that from a child's point of view, even a stubbed toe can seem like the end of the world. And if Mommy wasn't available at just the right moment to kiss the boo-boo, that's an even scarier moment for the child.

The sensitive-hearted experience more inner strength than those with bruised hearts. They present with a sense of purpose. "I survived daily criticism from my father," a young man might say, "therefore I can handle anything." They also tend to deny just how bad it really was for them.

Unlike the passive stance of the bruised heart, sensitive-heart mentality is survival-oriented and active. Nevertheless, the survivor remains a prisoner. Because the aim of sensitive-heart mentality is to prevent the occurrence of further insults, growth and thriving are not necessarily supported.

Sensitive-heart mentality may be quite useful for the journey out of a childhood filled with neglect, toxic dysfunction, or abuse, but it has limited value for an adult seeking a healthy-hearted existence. Those with a sensitive-heart mentality remain inadequately equipped for life's curve balls.

The sensitive-hearted are not really living in the present. They expend too much time and energy warding off things that are unlikely to happen. Paradoxically, they don't have adult strategies for dealing with actual injustices in the present. They tend to focus on figuring out how others will hurt them. Consequently, they may miss out on the delights of meeting new people. They seem strong but lack flexibility. While much better off than the bruised-hearted, who exist in maximum-security psychological prisons, those with sensitive hearts are still compelled toward certain reactions rather than propelled by choice.

Those with bruised hearts who become sensitive-hearted often mistakenly believe their healing is done. They may become giddy with a new sense of empowerment. But even with a sensitive heart as I describe it here, they're still trapped by the wounds of the past, and their self-definition remains linked to a bruised heart. They become the survivors of a bruised heart—therefore, they're still not free.

The sensitive-hearted minimize the true pleasures of the world that are right at their fingertips. If their heart remains sensitive in this way, such people may lack true zest for life, resigned that having been victimized has forever damaged the core of their being. They can never seem to stop and breathe and fully recognize their special gifts. Who they are and what they've done will never be enough to fill the hole or to make them feel whole.

Unless they continue on a healing path, these people remain at serious risk for revictimizing themselves, especially by re-creating emotional wounds in their adult relationships. They still need to heal from the damage they knowingly or unknowingly inflict upon themselves when reliving childhood patterns.

THE THRIVING HEALTHY-HEART

Thrivers grow vigorously. They flourish. To Thrivers, the glass is half full, not half empty. They know how to fill the glass the rest of the way if they so choose. They know where to empty the glass if they don't like what's in it and how to start over. They have excitement and enthusiasm. They neither seek out problems nor avoid them. They are independent yet unafraid to ask for help. They can discriminate between safe and unsafe people. If their requests for help are refused, they know how to modify the request or seek a new source. They have the judgment to ask for help appropriately. They neither mistreat others nor tolerate mistreatment. They seek win-win situations.

Those who become Thrivers transform and integrate the painful remnants of their past into gifts. They transform trauma into treasure, adversity into challenge, and suffering into empathy. Thrivers do not let previous negative experiences affect their optimism toward future experience. They don't assume all relationships will be difficult and heartbreaking just because they may have been in ones that were.

Thrivers exhibit deep compassion for others without sacrificing themselves. While never happy about the suffering they endured, they heal from it. They don't define their identities by it, and they genuinely like themselves. They exude confidence without being arrogant. Whether by becoming therapists, teachers, artists, screenwriters, lawyers, secretaries, computer analysts, by becoming excellent parents or partners, or by volunteering their services to help others, they contribute solutions.

The biggest distinguishing feature of Thrivers is their awareness of choice, even when all the available options stink! In this mode, they see themselves as making an impact on the world. They take control of the things they truly have control over, like their behavior. And they recognize the areas where they have no power, such as their inability to change other people's behavior.

Thrivers have room to take responsibility for their actions. They are aware of how their choices affect other people. On the other hand, they recognize the difference between feeling responsible for other people's behavior and knowing how to accept their influence, without taking ownership of others' feelings.

Thrivers know how to say "NO!" to mistreatment and "YES!" to love, comfort, excitement, happiness, and passion.

As a Thriver, when you step on someone's toes, you're not ashamed to apologize. You don't go out of your way to hurt others, yet you don't censor yourself simply to protect another's feelings, whatever the feelings may be. You create a balance between thinking of yourself and taking into account the needs and opinions of others whom you care about.

Sounds pretty good, doesn't it? It's understandable, however, for someone to not yet be able to relate to this way of being. After all, until now your wounds have inhibited you from learning how to thrive. Thriving is a whole new and different experience from what you're used to. It's an entirely different complex of behavior, belief, and feeling. At the same time, it's one that anybody can embody if they set their mind to it and change their behavior. So right now, make a statement to yourself that you want and deserve to thrive. It's your inherent right. The moment you invite it, you open the door to welcoming it in and living in your most natural state.

Take a moment and identify for yourself how you believe you've been living your life—more like a bruised or sensitive heart or more like a Thriver. This isn't an exact science, so there's no need to put yourself into a box by choosing only one of the three. Most often, you will discover that your orientation to the world shifts depending on your level of stress, how well you care for yourself, the quality of your support network at any given time, and so on.

WHAT IS REVICTIMIZATION, ANYWAY?

In order to approach life as a Thriver, it's essential that you understand the process of revictimization. Once you do, the deck is stacked in favor of your achieving "Thriverhood." If you don't reach this understanding, you'll remain unaware of what's really happening, which will reduce your ability to choose. That, of course, keeps you entrenched in either bruised- or sensitive-heart mentality.

Revictimization usually happens without your conscious awareness. It's the process of putting yourself in situations where you end up reliving your childhood pain and suffering. Without knowing it, you are driving on a collision course. No matter which way you turn or how cleverly you try to alter your route, you continue to crash into brick walls. You get injured over and over again. But because you don't fully recognize your role in the creation of the crash or your power to choose a better alternative, you lack the necessary equipment to successfully change the course itself.

Remember Cathy, who was convinced that she only attracted guys who didn't like women? She absolutely believed that her relationships chose her. Cathy never even saw the option to not get involved in the first place, even when she came face to face with red flags.

Bill, her last boyfriend, professed his undying love, but his actions failed to match his words. He rarely arrived on time for their dates. He insulted and degraded her when he didn't get his way, and he made fun of her vulnerabilities in front of his friends. Despite his abominable treatment of her. She would do his laundry, run errands to free up his time, and buy thoughtful gifts to say "I love you." He never offered his help with things she needed to accomplish yet continued to demand her good will. Throughout it all, Cathy figured she could transform Bill into a man who sees the value in women. No such luck!

Even when she consistently felt hurt and betrayed, once involved, Cathy never took the initiative in ending her troublesome relationships. Despite the perpetual mistreatment, she would wait until the guy ended the affair. While not initially obvious, Cathy was reenacting a wound from her childhood.

Her father, although in some ways outwardly loving and supportive of Cathy's endeavors, had a very sexist view of women. He didn't overtly abuse Cathy or her mother, but he insinuated that women should be submissive to men and relegate their needs to their husbands' desires. Cathy never developed an appreciation for her inner worth. But while she correctly identified herself as a magnet for men who would disrespect and devalue her importance, she incorrectly assumed a fatalistic posture about it.

Annette's story illustrates a most extreme example of self-inflicted victimization. Between the ages of twenty-one and thirty, she had been the victim of two violent crimes. She was in no way at fault for the actual criminal acts inflicted upon her. At the same time, she bore some responsibility for their occurrence. In both cases, when we examined the course leading up to the incidents, we discovered a complete disregard for her primary safety needs. Unintentionally, Annette had put herself in risky situations where the probability of being a victim increased tremendously.

In one incident, Annette's boss asked her to work late. Though a security guard offered to escort her to her car located deep within a dark parking structure, she didn't feel entitled to "burden" the guard. So she walked to her car alone. Tragically Annette was robbed along the way. While there is no guarantee that making different choices would have prevented the attack, the probability of her being robbed would certainly have been reduced had she allowed the guard to escort her.

Annette's parents divorced when she was five, and she rarely saw her father again. Her mother, feeling extremely burdened by single motherhood, had very little ability to self-care and very limited parenting skill. Because Annette's mother didn't place safety needs as a priority, Annette failed to learn the basic lessons about how to keep out of danger. What she did learn, unfortunately, was not to bother other people with her problems and therefore not to ask for help. Both her tendency to be self-punitive and the absence of any entitlement to rely on others for assistance, even when her safety was at stake, set her up to be an easy target for victimization.

Sensitive-hearted adults can revictimize themselves in many ways. Some may deprive their bodies of necessary rest, sleep, or food. Some may ignore necessary emotional supplies like nurturing, kindness, acceptance, and self-valuation. Some deprive themselves of essential social interaction by becoming isolated and by retreating into solitude. Others deprive themselves of necessary space and separateness by constantly surrounding themselves with people or work. Some overtly degrade and downright abuse themselves. They call themselves insulting names like "stupid" or "idiot." They intentionally injure themselves physically. They punish themselves when they fail to do something perfectly.

Others indirectly perpetuate their wounds by adopting ineffective methods of expressing needs. Some wait so long to acknowledge what they need that, by the time they're aware, they've become so angry and deprived that they get enraged at those who might actually be able and willing to help fulfill their needs. Or they look toward others to meet needs that they are entirely capable of meeting on their own.

Paul overworked himself for many consecutive months at his job and desperately needed a vacation. In fact, he accrued an extra five days of vacation time as a result of all the overtime he put in. But rather than ask for the time off that he had clearly earned, he waited for his boss to tell him to go ahead and take time off. You can see where this is going. His boss never offered him a vacation, not because he believed Paul shouldn't have one, but because he was too darn busy and overworked himself to even notice his own needs, let alone Paul's.

In Paul's history, his father taught him to believe that when people really respect you, they will go out of their way to take care of you. Because Paul's boss never noticed his exhaustion, and because Paul hadn't learned that it was his own job to take care of his needs, he became burnt out and resentful of his employer.

Another very common way for people to revictimize themselves is to expect that others can read their minds. Janice, for example, never observed her parents asking directly for what they wanted or needed from each other. Her mother, in particular, didn't feel she had a right to her own needs, so she would try to manipulate Janice's father into giving her what she wanted. The father would usually just get annoyed and would then withhold love. Janice grew into adulthood like her mother, not knowing how to openly and directly express her needs.

When she got married, she expected her husband to guess what she wanted. But, of course, he was never right. Though she meant well, he couldn't possibly succeed because he didn't have the essential information from her as to how to please her. In her mind, he continually disappointed her on purpose. She became increasingly resentful. She had no idea that this expectation was basically destroying the potential for actually getting at least some of what she needed from her husband. Because of her expectation that her husband should accurately read her mind, she didn't see that it was her responsibility to speak up in order to have a healthy relationship. Unfortunately for Janice, by the time she realized this, it was too late. Her husband divorced her because he felt trapped in a double bind. She had unwittingly placed him in a no-win situation. However, while the divorce devastated and reinjured her emotionally, it inspired her to get some help. Once she did, she was able to see that she had been unconsciously perpetuating her own despair. With this recognition, she began to realize that she had the power to choose something else, like speaking up.

Like Cathy, you may not be convinced that you have real choices about the people you pick for social and intimate relationships. And like Annette, you may be so unfamiliar with how to best care for your own needs that you even miss those involving your physical safety. Or like Paul or Janice, it's possible you haven't learned that it's your own job to get your needs met.

All these sensitive-hearted people needed to discover that, unbeknownst to them, they actually created scenarios that increased the probability of further wounding. They needed to awaken their power of choice.

THE POWER OF CHOICE

Recognizing your power to choose is the most fundamental component for stopping the revictimization process. As we move toward health, we learn to make better, more life-affirming choices. Once you claim this power, you will be in charge of your feelings and actions. You will actually decrease your tendency to mistreat yourself and to draw into your world others who may mistreat you. If you reduce your vulnerability to predators, you also reduce the predator's interest in you. It's that simple. If you no longer hold yourself out as prey, you won't be preyed upon. You'll exude a "No Predators Allowed" stance without even having to verbalize it. You'll become a magnet for nurturing relationships.

When people feel they've been mistreated as children, they often fail to develop a belief in their power to choose. They often believe that good things only happen by chance. And to make matters worse, they also believe that they cause the bad things that happen. What a horrible double bind. No credit for the good stuff, and all the blame for the yuck!

Conversely, adults who felt they were nurtured and loved in childhood tend to develop a healthy sense of self-responsibility. They can take credit for the good stuff and can even claim the not-so-good when they actually have responsibility for it. Claiming your power to choose will enable you to bring in the love you deserve, both from yourself and from others.

MOVING INTO HEALING

In the chapters that follow, we examine the eleven steps towards healing, three stages of growth and change.

In the first stage, you'll learn to embrace the whole of who you are today, both your strengths and limitations. You will become your own best friend and companion.

In the second stage, you'll relive your past and the wounds you've been housing, but not from the perspective of a frightened child. You'll dive into the stuff that keeps you threatened and self-sabotaging, with a safety net.

In the third stage, you'll learn to embrace your power to choose and your inherent right to thrive. You'll maximize the gifts and strengths that are fully yours to enjoy because of your total life experience.

Chapter Five

Step One:
Celebrate Your Strength

Most people with leftover wounds and sensitive hearts have difficulty seeing how amazing they are for having lived with their hurt for so long. The journey toward a healthy heart begins by identifying and celebrating your strengths, accomplishments, and resources, no matter how insignificant they may seem. If nothing else, you must congratulate yourself on having made it this far.

The fact that you live and breathe and continue to yearn for growth deserves to be honored. If you're anything like the many people I've worked with, you may not believe you deserve recognition for simply being. Whether taught by parents, teachers, or society at large, you may feel entitled to recognition only for achieving or accomplishing something great. Your self-worth has become based on what you do, not on who you are as a person. This conditional love for yourself has got to stop.

Acceptance of your whole being, including both your prized and not-so-prized character traits, does not mean that you cannot change things about yourself if you want to. Acceptance is not the same as resignation. Rather it is the prerequisite for change, if you so desire, and essential for happiness. But first you must treasure and appreciate your whole self as is. You must come to equally value your accomplishments and strengths as well as your failures, mistakes, and limitations.

Believe it or not, everything you've endured throughout your life, from the very beginning up to this moment in time,

can become a resource for you. While it might be very difficult at this point to consider that the hurt you've carried can
actually become a gift, I strongly encourage you to embrace
this notion.

I certainly wish you no harm or further injury. Yet all experiences have value. Essentially, like a diamond in the rough, you
can transform any negative experience into a positive asset.
Anything can be turned into a positive if you fully embrace your
experience and your suffering with love and respect. That
doesn't mean you deserved to suffer. Quite the contrary. It's my
hope and goal that you will continue to suffer less and less as
you do your healing. Once you can claim this new perspective,
you'll no longer feel damaged by the wounds you've endured.
Rather, you will become more and more enriched and better
equipped to deal with the trials and tribulations of daily life as
well as with crisis and stress.

Actually, our pain and suffering permit us the experience of
empathy and compassion. Many of you may have an easier time
providing compassion for others. Because you may believe you
don't deserve compassion, you might not know how to give it
to yourself. You might be waiting and hoping that the world will
provide it for you, only to be disappointed that others don't,
can't, or won't. Even when you do receive compassion from
others or provide it for yourself, it doesn't seem to stick. You
don't yet have any place to store it. You must develop a con-
tainer for compassion.

WEAVING A CLOAK OF COMPASSION

Close your eyes and visualize yourself weaving a protective gar-
ment of beautiful silk or soft wool. Embroider upon it the
words "Compassion for Me." Then wrap yourself snugly within
this protective cloak. This is where you will keep love, acceptance, and compassion close to your heart. You needn't wait for

anyone else to give these to you. You have the power to give to yourself all of the compassion you'll ever need.

Melinda initially sought therapy to deal with career issues. She liked her job in human resources and constantly received praise and acknowledgment for her performance. But at the end of each day, she experienced a longing for more. It didn't make sense to her why she wasn't more content.

In childhood Melinda invested all her energy in getting good grades and pleasing her parents in order to receive their approval. While her parents believed they were helping her develop high self-esteem by praising her successes, they didn't realize that they often failed to acknowledge her when she was just hanging out. Although they certainly didn't abuse her, they didn't understand the value in demonstratively loving their child even when she was doing nothing.

Melinda's father, in particular, defined his value by his success at his work. His father had treated him as worthless when he wasn't being productive. He would call him names like "lazy" and "good for nothing." Melinda's father in no way meant to pass this along to his daughter. In fact, he intended to give her positive recognition. But unfortunately, Melinda's self-worth also became based on her achievements. What she really longed for was to feel loved for the genuinely kind and gentle person she is.

While somewhat fulfilling, the praise she received at work couldn't satisfy her longing for basic acceptance of her existence. When Melinda wasn't doing a good job at something, she often became depressed and devaluing of herself. However, with her growing awareness of this need, she learned to be appreciative of the inner qualities that make her who she is, not just her outward accomplishments.

It's not enough to acknowledge who you are. You must truly celebrate and honor yourself for having made it this far. Carrying around unfinished business is a tedious task. It has probably burdened you far more than you're even aware.

Remember, as a child you have to make the best of what is offered to you. And if you don't learn anything different, you will flock toward what's most familiar. You'll unknowingly create experiences that reinforce your methods of coping. While the ways you learned to live have serviced your survival in the past, now it's time to come back to your inherent nature to thrive. And thriving requires that you see yourself clearly through loving and accepting eyes.

CELEBRATING YOU: A CEREMONY

Now you will do an exercise involving the identification of all your qualities that best describe you, including those you consider to be positive as well as those you consider to be negative. However, in order for this to be a meaningful process, it is very important that you create a calm and serene atmosphere. Take a minute to check your surroundings. Are you in a quiet, relaxed setting? Will you be interrupted by the ringing of the telephone; the needs of your children, pets, or friends; the demands of your boss; or the chatter in your head about the "things to do today" list? If distractions are likely, you're better off rethinking whether this is the most opportune moment to continue or if there may be a more beneficial time later in the day. While I'm certainly not advocating procrastination, usually it's more advantageous to create a better time than to jump in impulsively at a time when you probably won't accomplish much, if anything. The last thing you want to create is a situation where you will be interrupted and potentially feel cheated out of something you want. That would not be in service of your healing adventure. Instead create a situation where you'll have the highest probability of achieving your goals. You may be so familiar with things not going the way you desire, envision, or expect that you may not even recognize your own role in creating the disappointing outcomes.

For instance, if you're reading this between business meetings, while preoccupied with a particular deadline or unfinished task, or when completely exhausted, you'll be more likely to miss essential information or even forget everything you just read. On the other hand, if you devote a block of time specifically for this exercise, are reasonably rested, and eliminate any foreseeable interruptions, you're more likely to benefit from the process.

Take a minute to decide if this is the best moment to proceed. If you have a chunk of time, make sure you reduce distractions. Turn on the answering machine, let others know you will be busy for a certain period of time, or go to a place where no one you know is likely to be. Dedicate this time to yourself. By making time for doing this exercise and others throughout the book, you'll be firmly stating that you value yourself. You'll be ending the vicious cycle of revictimization and paving the way for thriving.

Most of us grow to value certain qualities over others, depending upon what qualities our caregivers or other important individuals or institutions value. By the time we're adults, we have a positive or negative value associated with any given characteristic. For instance, when you hear the word "submissive," what value do you place on that quality? Would you like to be viewed by others as submissive? Would it make a difference if the term was used to describe a man versus a woman? What about "aggressive"? Would it be a compliment or an insult to be called aggressive?

Hopefully the following exercise will increase your awareness of the qualities you possess. It will help you identify the value, positive or negative, you have attached to each. Then I'll help you neutralize the value judgment so that you can more easily claim all aspects of yourself. After all, it's very hard to acknowledge something about yourself if it has a very negative connotation. Or if you're able to acknowledge it, it's still hard to appreciate qualities that you perceive to be negative.

I hope that you can begin to think in terms of how effective certain qualities may be rather than whether they are good or bad, positive or negative.

- Step One: Make a list of all the qualities you possess that you judge to be positive.
- Step Two: Make a list of all your qualities you judge to be negative.
- Step Three: Using your list of positives, identify a situation in your life where having the opposite of one of these qualities may have served you better. Then take your list of negatives and think of a situation where having this quality is actually to your advantage.

Below is a list of some of the qualities that, in our culture, people generally deem either dominantly positive or negative. Please note, however, that your personal history and the attitudes of those who influenced your development will uniquely determine how you value these qualities. The list is not comprehensive, so please use it as a guide not a prescription.

POSITIVE QUALITIES

GENDER NEUTRAL
assertive, confident, considerate, curious, dedicated, dependable, determined, energetic, funny, happy, honest, humble, kind, patient, persistent, playful, relaxed, reliable, sincere, smart, thoughtful

FEMALE ASSOCIATED
expressive, gentle, selfless, sensitive, sweet

MALE ASSOCIATED
adventurous, hard working, strong

NEGATIVE QUALITIES

aggressive, angry, arrogant, cautious, emotional, hostile, impulsive, inconsiderate, irresponsible, lazy, manipulative, passive, selfish, serious, stubborn, unreliable, weak

Our judgments prohibit us from truly appreciating ourselves. Clearly, if you only see the value in one side of a quality and not in its opposite, you are restricting your being. We all have the capacity to embody the full range of these qualities if we welcome and permit them to exist. But most of us don't have the internal permission to claim the full range.

I could give examples of how each of the qualities called positive actually wouldn't be so positive in certain situations. I could also demonstrate how each of the so-called negative would be very adaptive under different conditions. Every one of our qualities has the potential to serve us well or to limit us, depending on the circumstances. Rather than offering a long list of examples, I think that by highlighting a few of the most loaded ones, you'll see what I'm talking about.

Teresa grew up believing that girls should not outshine boys, especially in sports. Although she was a great athlete, by the time she was a teenager, she had restricted her talents so as not to be rejected by the boys at school. She became less outgoing and more quiet and passive. She truly believed she would not be as well liked if she openly demonstrated her more boisterous self.

Later in life, she encountered numerous occasions where being able to express herself more openly would have been to her advantage. She had a boss who tended to pick on her and devalue her achievements because her success threatened his self-esteem. He needed to appear smarter and more competent. Because Teresa had learned to contain and hide her assertiveness, she stayed far too long in a job where she was very unfulfilled.

It never occurred to Teresa that she had other options, like confronting him, going to his superior, or simply quitting and finding a more satisfying situation. When she finally accepted that she had the capacity to assert herself, she recognized how doing so would serve her better in many situations. She could then see past her fear of rejection and reclaim her right to overt expression.

Margaret came from a family of heavy-duty scientific intellectuals. Her father was an astronomer, her mother was an electrical engineer, and her brother was a pharmaceutical researcher. Margaret was the more creative, far less brainy member of the bunch. Though her parents loved her, they had no idea what to do with her. They preferred a challenging game of Trivial Pursuit, while Margaret's creative spirit drew her toward writing stories about little children. Over the years, her parents became increasingly distant. They didn't know how to relate to her.

Eventually Margaret sold out to the pressures of her family milieu. She studied hard in school and became an accountant. All professions have a creative component, but this was a far cry from her life's energy. She had grown to view her creativity not as a gift but more of a weakness.

Years later, Margaret had a family of her own and one of her children manifested extraordinary creative talent. Her child touched her heart in many ways, and Margaret discovered her own creativity waiting eagerly to emerge. Once she was able to get past her fears of reclaiming her creativity, she was able to use it to the fullest potential with her daughter. Voilá, her limitation was transformed into strength, an amazing and wonderful outcome for both Margaret and her daughter. Margaret's creative energy had actually always been a resource; she just wasn't able to experience it that way, having viewed it through the eyes of her caregivers. And those eyes, if you recall, weren't able to value it.

Joe's story involves the quality of sensitivity. His father teased him relentlessly as a little boy whenever Joe felt touched by something, especially if Joe cried. He got the stereotypical line: "Big boys don't cry, only girls and sissies do." Because he wanted to keep his father's approval, he learned very early on that he better buck up and keep his feelings contained.

When Joe married, his wife constantly complained that he never demonstrated affection or softness. She wanted a kind and caring man and truly welcomed his sensitivity. As a lawyer, his ability to keep his feelings contained worked well for him in the courtroom, but it debilitated his capacity to have the loving relationship his wife begged him for. He eventually understood that there was a valuable place for his sensitivity. Fortunately for him, his realization came before his wife was ready to call it quits.

One quality in particular that makes many people cringe is "manipulative." Who in their right mind wants to be called that? Whenever it's used to describe someone, the term almost always carries a negative connotation. But let's face it: we're all manipulative at times, and what's really so bad about that? If you always try to get what you need or want by manipulating or exploiting others, it would be better to learn other, more direct ways of self-fulfillment. But in many situations, knowing how to manipulate can be a remarkably effective tool.

One young woman I treated, Sandra, recognized that while she loved her husband and was happy with him, he wasn't the best at sharing his feelings. He had no interest in developing this capacity. Though she would have preferred a husband who could share his feelings more easily, she wasn't bothered enough to contemplate leaving. However, she did notice that under certain circumstances, he would more readily expose his emotional life, like when he was really relaxed and unburdened by his enormous job responsibilities.

Sandra learned that whenever she had something really important to discuss with her husband, it served her best to create an atmosphere that would be most conducive to getting her needs met; that is, to have him share his feelings. This was a conscious manipulation on her part. He was never harmed in the process, didn't really know it was happening, and, along with Sandra, he gained something in the process. Her attempts to go through the front door usually failed, so she found more welcoming back doors. In this case, manipulation could also be termed positive, creative persuasion.

I hope these examples help you see that there's a place in the world for all qualities, even those that may initially create a strong negative reaction. For instance, while I'm certainly not advocating that it's okay for people to abuse others, it's still valuable to embrace your capacity for aggression. Aggression has a time and place, too. This is not permission to randomly act out your impulses if they will intentionally hurt or exploit others. Behavior is a whole different story. We need to be accountable and responsible for our behavior, but we must be careful not to equate our inner world with our outer actions.

Once you've made your list of positives and negatives, cross out those headings. You'll now be unifying both lists into a set of qualities you accept about yourself that sometimes work to your advantage and sometimes to your disadvantage. Knowing and accepting all of your qualities gives you more power to choose your behavior.

Next, it's time to identify and celebrate your accomplishments. List them all, no matter how small they may seem to you. If you have trouble, ask yourself what someone who loves you (such as a friend, family member, or mate) would put on the list. Include successes that no one knows about along with those you've shared with others. Include achievements for both long-term and short-term goals. Don't be afraid to be boastful. Being boastful requires someone else present to perceive you as boastful. Come on! It's a great opportunity to feel good about yourself. Why not take it?

As usual, the last step is not the least. Just as it's important to acknowledge the qualities in yourself that you perceive to be positive, you also need to acknowledge mistakes and even failures. These do not have to be negative. Limitations, failures, and mistakes are part of the human condition. Whatever you were taught that led you to believe that you must succeed at everything has got to be thrown out. It's not realistic and won't help you heal. You probably won't believe me now, but I hope that as you see the healing process unfold throughout each stage, eventually you'll agree.

Take a moment and do an inventory. What have you been trying to achieve, without success? What qualities do you think get in the way of achieving those things? What do you need to develop or improve in yourself to make those things happen? Most importantly, whom will you please if you achieve these goals? Who will you disappoint if you don't?

As an adult, you've probably become you own worst critic. Vow to be gentle, kind, and loving toward yourself. A loving touch goes a lot further than a whack on the head with a hammer. Love and nurturing help us grow and flourish. Harshness and ridicule only create more injury and won't motivate change.

Chapter Six

Step Two:
Acknowledge Your Wounds

Many people cannot see beyond the wounds of the past. Others have either buried all memory or recognition of emotional pain or refused to see the point in acknowledging something that has already happened. To move forward, however, anything left unhealed must be acknowledged, regardless of whether the specific events that caused the pain can be recalled. Since you've picked up this book, at least a part of you recognizes that something unhealed desires resolution and closure.

In Step Two of the healing process, you explore the specific wounds of your past and learn to offer compassion and empathy for the hurt. It doesn't matter whether the wounds were inflicted intentionally or unintentionally. The only thing that matters is the end result.

Before we get started, I'd like you to do two very important things. This may seem silly at first, but it's important. First, have a pep talk with your sensitive self. Second, develop an image of protection to facilitate a safe journey through the tunnel of your childhood.

PEP TALK

Imagine yourself comforting and soothing a young child who is upset. In this case, the child is your own vulnerable self. Practice saying the following.

Okay, my precious self, we're going on a journey through what might be a dark tunnel. We may experience discomfort and even pain. This is like getting an immunization shot. Even though the shot may sting, the long-term benefit is worth it. In order to heal and move toward thriving, we must acknowledge the pain that is already there. By uncovering it, we have the best chance of letting it go so it will no longer burden us. This is not the same as dwelling on something. Rather, it's a means to transforming what is now an unwanted experience into something to treasure and embrace. All my experience creates who I am.

PROTECTIVE IMAGE

Because many of our sensitivities from childhood have collected a lot of dust over the years, uncovering them can sometimes feel quite overwhelming and even scary. So it's crucial to build up as much of a sense of safety and protection as possible. We do this not in the way we have armored ourselves in the past, with a false sense of protection, but in a way that truly provides security. You'll have to decide for yourself what that image is for you, but I've provided a suggestion that might at least give you some ideas.

Choose an animal that represents strength and courage, like a lioness or bear. Next, choose one that represents peace and serenity like a deer, dove, or swan. You'll need the balance of both these resources to center you as you acknowledge your wounds. Once you've chosen your animals, picture one on your right shoulder and one on your left. Invite them to stay with you at all times.

If you don't relate to the animal images, feel free to choose some other symbol, like a character from a story or a real person you admire, to embody these qualities. You might even select a memory of yourself at a time when you felt fully anchored to your strength and inner peace.

Remember, Thrivers use all available resources. So make sure you pad yourself with as much support as possible. You can never have too much support. If you have more than you need at any given time, you're in a far better position than if you don't have enough. When you have more than enough, you simply don't have to use the extra.

THROUGH THE TUNNEL OF CHILDHOOD

To recover your full power to thrive, you will have to undertake what may be a dark journey. This may be unpleasant or even downright painful at times. Please remember that going through the darkness will allow you to completely embrace the beautiful vista at the other end. Don't give up. Memories are memories, not current events. They aren't happening in the present. They can no longer hurt you once you claim your power to turn off the pain.

If you're holding onto a lot of pain, especially if you are not well aware of it because of having developed self-protective guards, it can be extremely difficult to make contact with your sensitive heart. Below are several activities that may facilitate a connection to your vulnerable self.

EXERCISE 1—USING PHOTOGRAPHS TO RECONNECT WITH YOUR CHILDHOOD MEMORIES

Find pictures of yourself from your early years, preferably from infancy through your teens. Don't worry if you can't find a picture for each year. Find what you can. You'll also need a pad and pencil to write your thoughts and feelings. Please allot ample time to do this exercise, taking thirty or forty minutes during which you won't be interrupted. If you don't have that kind of time now, you can always come back and do this later.

Start with the most recent photo. Take a close look. Write down what you see. Pay attention to how you look, your expression, who you are with, the time of year, where you are, and so on. Ask yourself about the dominant emotions the photo evokes. Let yourself wander through your mental images. If any memories emerge, try to recall them in detail. Journal as much as you can from that period of your life, making sure to focus on both the pleasant and unpleasant aspects. If you experience strong emotions of sadness, anger, fear, or joy, be sure to note these. Also pay close attention to your body for any signs of shame.

Jimmy's experience provides a good example. Jimmy was thirty-seven at the time he came for therapy. He looked back at a photo of himself at his high school prom. His initial recollection was joyful, but then he quickly flashed to another scene. Before the big night, he had gotten into a huge fight with his father about borrowing the car. His father told him he could have the car as long as he returned it by eleven. Jimmy knew his friends would be out much later than that. He thought his father was being unreasonable, given the special occasion.

Jimmy felt helpless. He knew his father wouldn't change his mind. His father already thought Jimmy was spoiled for wanting things the father didn't think he should have. When Jimmy tried to negotiate, his father told him that if he didn't "knock it off" he'd get nothing. Jimmy could have argued, but he knew that at best he might get an extra half an hour with the car at the price of suffering his father's wrath for days to come about his ingratitude.

While the father's strictness certainly had benefits in terms of teaching Jimmy responsibility, respect, and the ability to delay gratification, at times he was overly harsh and insensitive to special circumstances. His style of teaching these values and his inflexibility created a deep wound in Jimmy. Jimmy hadn't thought about this memory for years and had no conscious connection to the anger and resentment. But once he looked at his prom pictures, he discovered strong emotions still quite alive.

Like Jimmy, your unhealed wounds may become apparent only once your memory is jogged. Choose one event at a time, and keep doing this exercise as needed. You may notice that you have fewer conscious memories as you go back further in time. But feelings may still be evoked when you look upon your younger years, even if you have little or no memory of a context. A picture of yourself at your fourth birthday party may make you feel sad, though you don't know why. That's perfectly all right. Just notice the feelings and write about whatever you do recall. Don't judge them, and stay curious. You don't have to do this all at once, especially if you have many photos or many unhealed wounds. Set a pace you can tolerate. If you experience intense emotion, go slowly. Be careful not to overwhelm yourself. The purpose of this exercise is to help you make a connection to your sensitive self, not to send yourself deeper into hiding.

Exercise 2—Creating a New Dialogue with Your Sensitive Heart

Pick a picture of yourself at a young age, and place it somewhere where you will see it several times a day, like in your car, on your desk at work, or on your dresser or bathroom mirror. Put a picture in several locations if you can, but start with at least one. Make it a ritual to say "hello" to yourself in the picture at least three times daily. If you feel silly, just keep practicing. As you get more comfortable with saying hello, expand the dialogue. Have an actual conversation with yourself. The picture serves as a reminder of your vulnerability. If you don't need the picture to remind you of this, then you're already a step ahead and you can just use mental images instead.

When you talk to yourself, do so in a manner you wish others had used with you when you were a child. Take the example of Kristen, who is a marketing rep for a large company. Her job description involves giving many presentations to large groups of people. Unfortunately, any kind of public speaking makes Kristen very nervous. Before seeking therapy, she dealt with her anxiety with harshness and insensitivity. She typically responded to her fear with irritation, telling herself, with no empathy, "Get over it, it's no big deal, you're such a big baby for being nervous." In fact, this response only served to alienate her more from her needs.

What Kristen didn't know was that by not giving herself support or compassion, she was eliminating any opportunity to work through her nervousness. She later revealed that she was simply copying her mother's attitude towards her.

Kristen recalled a time when she had to give her first oral report at school. She was very nervous about speaking aloud in front of her peers, and she told her mother, hoping for comfort. Her mother, however, treated Kristen as though she were making a mountain out of a molehill. Rather than soothing Kristen's fear, her mother dismissed her daughter's feelings and shamed her in the process.

Once Kristen learned to speak to her anxiety with the comfort and empathy she longed for, she not only felt better as an adult, but also served to heal the wound from childhood. Now when she gets nervous before a presentation, she says to herself, "Of course you're nervous about giving the presentation. That can be a scary process, especially when you feel you need others to like you. Let's see what I can do to make it less scary." This kind of dialogue allowed Kristen to actually work through her fear rather than exacerbate it and paved the way to her learning new tools, like relaxation exercises, meditation, and yoga.

EXERCISE 3—GUIDED IMAGERY

If you have someone you really trust, who cares about you, and who understands the value of emotional healing, you may want to enlist assistance from him or her to do this exercise. If not, you may want to record it or simply read through it a few times until you can ad lib from memory.

Find a comfortable place where you have privacy. Start by sitting in a chair or lying down with all your limbs uncrossed. Make sure the room temperature is warm enough to prevent getting too cold, as your body temperature will drop a little as you move through the relaxation process. Close your eyes and begin deep breathing, inhaling through your nose and exhaling through your mouth. If your nose is at all stuffed up, use your mouth for both inhaling and exhaling. As you do your breathing, imagine inhaling comfort and relaxation and exhaling all of your stress, tension, and worries.

Next, think of a color that you associate with a peaceful sensation. As you focus on the color, count backward from ten, becoming more and more relaxed with each number. If you feel relaxed when you reach the number one, proceed to the next step. If not, then redo the breathing technique until you do.

Once relaxed, imagine that you are traveling back to the home where you were raised. If you moved around a lot as a child, try to recall your earliest home. You are now reaching the front door. Stop for a moment and take a deep breath. Now you are reaching into your pocket for the key to the door. As you walk through the door, you feel complete acceptance of yourself and a willingness to meet head-on the memories of your childhood. You are about to reconnect with your young, more vulnerable self.

Now stop and take another deep breath. You see the little you, and you smile at yourself. Reach out your hand to take the hand of your little self. Feel the smallness of it and experience the vulnerability of a child. Tell your little self that you are going to take a long journey together that may be scary and uncomfortable at times, but that it's one you must take together. Now take another deep breath and pay attention to any feelings that have been elicited. Whatever the feeling is, simply note it and continue holding yourself without judgment. Breathe a sigh of relief. You have just started your journey with the whole of you.

Now take yourself to a place that brings you a sense of calm, maybe next to a waterfall, on the beach, or in a meadow with beautiful wildflowers. Make sure to also bring along the animal or other symbol you chose to represent peace. The place doesn't matter, just as long as it brings you a sense of tranquility. Once there in your imagination, say the following words: "I'm sorry if I have abandoned myself for so long. I promise to make every effort from now on to pay attention to myself and treat myself with kindness and respect. That may not always be easy, but I will promise to practice patience. I will love myself through all of my experiences and will continue to embrace my vulnerability and sensitivity."

Continue to imagine soothing yourself, and count from one to five. On one, take a deep breath. On two, notice your breath as you continue to be at peace. On three, exhale any tension. On four, continue to feel the comfort of your inner being as you slowly open your eyes. On five, open your eyes.

After you finish this exercise, take some time to reflect on it. Journal about it if you wish. Be playful and creative. Make a commitment to taking care of yourself through love and acceptance. You might even make a formal document adopting your whole self. Remember, what may seem silly to your rational adult self may be quite welcoming and healing to that part of you housing the old scars of the past. If you're really into playing with this concept, go ahead and set up a formal adoption ceremony with the parts of your being you have ignored or rejected.

The more willing you can become to make this connection to your self in total, the faster you'll be able to clear the obstacles to your thriving.

INVENTORY OF WOUNDS

Now it's time to do a full inventory of the wounds you've been carrying around. Keep your symbols of courage and strength with you at all times. Don't pressure yourself to do this in one sitting, especially if you endured chronic abuse or neglect in childhood. As I hope you've been learning, your healing is a process. It's not going to happen in a few hours.

You need to identify some basic elements of your story as best as your memory permits: what happened, by whom or what, and when. As you saw in the chapter on how unhealed wounds create sensitive hearts in children, this happens in a myriad of ways, including abuse in all its forms, dysfunction, mistreatment, deprivation of essential needs, prejudice, racism, or even by a mismatch in temperament between you and a caregiver.

It doesn't matter whether the wounds were intentionally or unintentionally inflicted. You can include everything that continues to hurt you, from infancy to the present. Though later on you will see that you probably had at least partial responsibility in creating the wounds you experienced in adulthood, for now just list them. Until you are conscious of how you have revictimized yourself, you won't fully know that you have the power to make other choices.

If this is the first time you have even entertained that notion that, as an adult, you're the one who primarily creates your own experience, the wounds you experienced as an adult will feel just as victimizing as those from childhood.

As you uncover these experiences, try to be a specific as possible. For instance, if you felt neglected by any of your important caregivers, try to expand on the specific events, places, and contexts that created this experience. Ask yourself what specific needs were neglected. Was it all the time or only when he or she was preoccupied? And how often was that?

Divide your paper into five columns: event, unresolved feeling, name of person, age or age range of occurrence, and what you need for resolution of the pain. Under the "event" column, specify in as much detail as possible the full context of what happened to you to create the wound.

Some of you may be worried or concerned that you are breaking a taboo by openly naming what happened. If so, please keep in mind that no one has to see your list, nor is this even about blame. You don't need to hate the people you felt hurt you, nor do you need to confront them or even change whatever relationship you happen to have with them now, if any.

You'll discover later on that you have many options about what to do once you acknowledge your wounds, but none of them are mandatory requirements. Give yourself free rein to express all that there is. Try not to censor or limit yourself in any way.

For the "unresolved feeling" column, specify the feeling(s) you still have whenever you recall the event. Keep the feelings in simple language if possible. There are four basic feelings: sad, mad, glad, and afraid. Of course our language gives us a long list of synonyms for the primary four, but for the purpose of this stage, try to stick to the basics. By the way, there are lots of words we use to define our feelings that actually don't. Take "rejection" for a moment. Often people say, "I feel rejected." In actuality, you can't feel rejected. You might notice that you have been rejected, but there is no universal feeling that comes along with rejection. I bet, if you think back in time, there have been occasions where you have been excluded from something and actually felt happy about it. So please be careful not to sell yourself a feeling that is actually a perception or thought about something. Really challenge yourself to get to the core.

For the "name of person" column, identify the primary person/people you connect to the wound. Don't limit the population to only family members. Lots of people and institutions affect our development. Our primary caregivers certainly have a dominant role in our sense of well-being, but many others share the burden of accountability, like teachers, coaches, relatives, and neighbors.

For the "age or age range" column, try to recall when the event started. If something transpired over a lengthy period, try to specify the age it started through the age the event no longer occurred. Some things, by the way, you'll probably notice haven't actually ended, but they may not be affecting you as deeply as they had when you were little. Or, if you haven't been able to heal certain wounds, the triggers may be just as intense. For instance, perhaps your parents had difficulty allowing you to express certain feelings. This is a pretty universal problem, and many people grow into adulthood without having experienced much support for the full range of their emotional life.

Therefore, every time you call your parents hoping for some emotional support, you may hear things like, "Oh don't worry so much, it's no big deal" or "Quit being so sensitive about that, you can't do anything to change it anyway." This kind of statement, while it means well, offers little in the way of empathy. You end the conversation no better off than you started. Chances are your parents aren't going to change their style. What you may not realize, though, is that you can learn to change your reaction to it.

Under the "what you need for resolution" column, go through each of the wounds you listed and ask yourself what would help you heal the pain. When you respond to your question, please don't censor any spontaneous wishes. You want to allow yourself the freedom to desire anything, even if it's not realistic.

Sally discovered that she most desired a heartfelt apology from her mother for all the times her mother blamed her for the things that were her mother's problems. But because of her mother's unwillingness to take responsibility for her own behavior, Sally would probably be waiting forever if she needed resolution to come from her mother. Yet an apology was what Sally yearned for.

While her mother would not provide the apology, Sally was able to come up with the next best solution through identification of what she needed—she could offer the apology to her own self. She actually didn't need her mother for this at all. So, again, don't judge what you yearn for, just acknowledge it. Later you'll learn, like Sally did, how to give the healing to yourself.

When you approach yourself with what you need to heal, use the following list as a guide: apology; acknowledgment; acceptance of responsibility for causing the wound (whether or not the intention was to harm); validation for your feelings and/or perceptions; or a change in behavior that supplies reassurance that the wound won't likely be reinflicted. (An example of the last case might be your drug-addicted brother, who verbally abuses you when under the influence of his drugs. You might need him to no longer use drugs and to go to an anger-management group.)

Though we often resort to fantasies of getting justice from or revenge on the people who have wounded us, especially if we believe they wounded us intentionally, this is rarely an effective method of resolution. However, you can certainly entertain your revenge fantasies in your own head as long as you don't act on them. Acting on them would only further complicate matters and would do nothing toward the goal of completion.

Try not to rush this exercise. I recommend you keep an ongoing journal. Add to your inventory as often as needed or as new memories surface. Sometimes, once you start a process of active uncovering, your memory will offer you more and more detail along the way. It's as though you have given yourself an invitation to fill you in on that which you may have unknowingly been rejecting.

Also, as you proceed through the steps, you may experience more and more willingness to face the demons of your past. Therefore, you'll want to do this exercise whenever you encounter a new level of self-acceptance.

Chapter Seven

Step Three:
End the "Do I/ Don't I Deserve It" Dance

For most of us, just acknowledging what happened won't make the pain go away. Our hearts will still remain sensitive. It helps, but it's insufficient for full healing. Childhood wounds so often leave us with a deep layer of self-doubt. Such doubt perpetually feeds a conscious or unconscious ambivalence about our worthiness to have all that we inherently deserve. We get trapped in the "Do I/Don't I Deserve It" Dance.

THE "DO I/DON'T I DESERVE IT" DANCE

Nothing debilitates our healing more than doubt about what we deserve. Sometimes this shows up as shame. I don't mean the kind of mild shame that is more closely akin to humility, healthy self-reflection, or conscientiousness. No, not the kind that reminds us of our humanity and capacity for less than good-natured will at times.

I'm talking about the kind of shame that says, "I don't deserve anything good." It's the kind that permeates the core of one's being. Sometimes the doubt creates less agony than shame, yet it still serves as a source of insecurity. When childhood wounds have created a self-doubting or shame-based existence, you'll be prone to evaluating your feelings, needs, thoughts, and behavior through a prism of self-loathing and self-criticism.

A self-doubting person perceives him or herself, at the core, to be unworthy of having basic human needs met, such as love, respect, attention, admiration, acceptance, pleasure, and/or comfort. He or she may even feel unworthy of basic survival needs like food, water, shelter, or physical warmth.

One young woman experienced such a level of unworthiness that, when the heater broke in her apartment, she didn't contact the apartment manager for an entire year because she didn't feel deserving of being warm.

While many people refer to shame or self-devaluation as a feeling, I prefer to differentiate it from the basic four (mad, glad, sad, or afraid). It's more of a state of being that actually interferes with the healthy experience of feelings. When in this state, there's often a lack of awareness of what you are feeling. If you are aware, you aren't free to express the feeling because the doubt wipes out permission to be your authentic self. It becomes like a roadblock to your body's natural destination.

The doubting of your worthiness becomes boundless and timeless. It begets more doubt or shame, initiating a negative spiral that can move you further away from growth, change, and, of course, the possibility of thriving. When shame or self-doubt intensifies, it can lead to devastating magnitudes manifested by suicidal thoughts.

Many people have this doubting process so ingrained they don't even recognize its existence. Often it just shows up in nonverbal ways. When Sally came for help, she manifested her feelings of unworthiness through her body language. When describing her history, she would lose eye contact with me, shrink down in her seat, become fidgety, have trouble articulating thoughts and feelings, and/or become silent. In her silence, there often lived a wish to disappear or become invisible. Sometimes she experienced a profound need to be comforted, but this wish produced even more distress, as she would question "Who am I to think I deserve comfort?"

There are many words used to convey this debilitating self-doubt, like embarrassment, humiliation, undeserving, unworthy, bad, defective, damaged, shameful, or unlovable. Take a moment and try to reflect on ways that you are prone to devaluing your worth and ultimately exacerbating your pain.

PAIN GUARDS

Some of you may wear your pain on your sleeve. You might suffer constant self-doubt, self-attack, and a pervasive sense that something is inherently wrong with you. But many of you, most likely, have created ways to put some distance between your buried pain and your actual conscious experience. Without even trying or knowing, you've successfully erected protective "pain guards" that act as shields from these states of debilitating self-doubt and devaluation.

These guards emerged to protect you from the depth of pain you no doubt felt from the experiences that wounded you in childhood. Had these not emerged, you would possibly be living in a constant state of duress and unable to carry out day-to-day challenges. These guards were once very important to your survival when you could not make free choices. In fact, those of you whose experiences may have prohibited you from developing these protective guards probably suffer more acutely and may have had a more difficult time fending off the daily stresses of adulthood. You may experience intensive reliving, in your mind and body, the wounds inflicted on you. You may have flashbacks, nightmares and intrusive memories, and thoughts of the emotionally and psychologically challenging situations you endured. At times, you may even lose track of time and have great difficulty distinguishing what happened to you in the past from what is happening in the present.

Remember these cover-ups emerged as a protection. Don't view them as something bad or useless. They served an essential function. Without them you would have become a complete mess and unable to function in the world. They permitted your continued development in the areas where you weren't being constantly thwarted. For instance, a young girl whose mother and father are too preoccupied with their own problems to focus enough attention on their daughter's needs may believe she has no one to turn to for help. To cope, she may dissociate herself from the pain of feeling neglected. In doing so, she permits herself the opportunity to excel at school and develop her intellect in a way that will help her create a sense of independence.

The only problem with these mechanisms is that, when you fully discover that you can heal the wounds of the past and create a relationship with yourself and the world devoid of further injury, the guards become obsolete. You won't need to throw them away, but you should put them up high on a shelf where they'll only be recycled in case of immediate danger.

Certain behavioral coping mechanisms also serve to keep the pain from shame, self-doubt, and devaluation out of consciousness. These include abuse of or addiction to drugs, alcohol, sex, food, gambling, self-inflicted injuries, deprivation of certain needs, and/or failure to self-care as a regular routine (such as bathing, getting enough sleep, or eating when hungry). If these apply to you, please pay close attention to the chapter devoted to healing your body.

Our minds are very creative. We are capable of creating an enormous range of pain guards. Some can be categorized as behaviors, like avoiding relationships, investing oneself in one activity at the exclusion of others, pretending things are no big deal, underachieving, overachieving, or perfectionism. Others are more like psychological defense mechanisms. They also have a behavioral component but are less observable and more about one's internal unconscious dynamics. These include emotional numbing, denial, projection, blaming, feeling/need replacement, intellectualization, grandiosity, and compensatory entitlement. Most likely these mechanisms emerge involuntarily and unconsciously. They are our body's way of compensating for things that happen to us that we have no control over.

As you read through the following descriptions and examples of the various pain guards, make special notes in the book or in a separate journal of the guards that seem to ring true to you. I can't emphasize enough how much it enhances awareness to take the extra step of writing down the personal relevance rather than just reading about it. Again, the bottom line to working through something is creating the fullest possible level of awareness, not just in your head but throughout your whole body. As you read, take the time to focus on and write about any feelings or memories that get activated. And for this phase, pay special attention to any experience of shame. Once you recognize your pain and how you've learned to defend against it, you have the power to choose something else. Whereas the bruised and sensitive-hearted are victims of their experience, Thrivers do their own choosing.

AVOIDING RELATIONSHIPS

One quite common way people keep themselves from experiencing the state of unworthiness is to avoid situations where this may occur. Since intimate relationships tend to elicit many feelings, if you can avoid them, you might not have to experience any form of shame. Maybe you believe that tender feelings are inherently shameful. What could be safer than to keep your emotional distance and not get close to someone in the first place? That way you have much less risk of being vulnerable. But your safety comes at a huge cost.

INVESTING IN ONE ACTIVITY AT THE EXCLUSION OF OTHERS

This can take many forms. For instance, you may spend most of your waking hours working, even though you have other obligations to your family. Maybe you feel inadequate as a parent but competent at your job. Or, if you really enjoy sports but you were teased as a child for insufficient athletic skills, you might reinvest this interest by compulsively watching sports rather than getting out there and having fun, regardless of your physical aptitude. This would protect you from having to face your internalized belief that you're deficient, hence avoiding any shame.

PRETENDING

With pretending, you essentially act like something is not as important to you as it actually is. For instance, your good friend talked about doing something special for your birthday. But when the big day arrived, he didn't even call because he had forgotten. If you're prone to self-doubt, it's likely that you don't fully believe you are worthy of having people go out of their way to make a special event for you. Rather than getting disappointed, hurt, or angry, you might pretend that it really doesn't matter to you that he forgot. You may even go so far as to not mention it when he does call.

By outwardly pretending that it's no big deal, you are attempting to convince yourself that your needs and feelings truly don't have importance. If successful, you're likely to avoid any self-consciousness or embarrassment you might have about them in the first place. In essence, if you render your needs and feelings unimportant and can convince yourself of this, then you'll have no reason to be ashamed.

UNDERACHIEVING

People who underachieve don't assert much effort toward improving their quality of life. This may take the form of procrastination or lack of motivation. It may be a means to avoid success and/or failure if you either believe you don't deserve success or if failure brings on feelings of inadequacy. This is not the same as being "laid back" or not being invested in the fast track of a capitalistic society. As a conscious choice, this attitude reflects acceptance. For many who are filled with self-doubt, on the other hand, underachieving may prevent the experience of shame. At the same time, it also prevents the pursuit of growth and change.

OVERACHIEVING

This mechanism can be particularly effective in preventing emotional pain if the internalized message in your self-concept is that "average" or "less that average" in any skill is equated with inadequacy or some kind of deficiency. If you constantly strive to achieve more and more, you won't have to face your limitations. Our highly competitive culture admires those who are achievement-oriented. But the quality loses its adaptive function when it's motivated by the need to avoid shame. It also becomes an especially debilitating mechanism when it creates chronic stress. Such stress may be manifested by physical symptoms (high blood pressure, dizziness, fatigue, rapid heart rate, ulcers, headaches, muscle spasms, to name a few) or psychological symptoms (such as being easily overwhelmed, anxiety, depression, preoccupation and/or chronic worry, never feeling a sense of completion, or the inability to relax).

Overachievers take on more than they can handle. It is like being in constant competition with oneself. Self-worth is based on what one does or achieves. With this behavioral coping style, there is little room to just be still, relax, and enjoy life. When this is driven by an internal sense of inadequacy or unworthiness, then any sense of pride from an accomplishment can only be short-lived. You become only as good as your last achievement. For healthy self-esteem, accomplishments can enhance an already good feeling about yourself. But, they cannot be the only supply of it.

PERFECTIONISM

Perfectionism is similar to overachieving but with an additional burden. Not only must one be constantly doing in order to experience worthiness, but one must also be doing everything flawlessly. The illusion for the perfectionist is that if you can meet everyone's expectations, no one will see how deeply flawed you believe yourself to be. But most of the time, the perfectionist is shooting to meet exceedingly high expectations that others don't actually have. I find it so terribly sad to watch someone in the throes of perfectionism struggle to catch a breath when faced with a failure or limitation. There's no way to ever meet everyone's expectations all of the time. The perfectionist never gets to rest. Perfect for one person might be a nightmare for someone else. There's just no way to win. Someone will inevitably be disappointed or dissatisfied.

EMOTIONAL NUMBING

Emotional numbing comes in two forms, either "push-down" or "split-off."

"Push-down numbing" is comparable to forgetting, but unlike the process of forgetting, whatever has been pushed down isn't actually lost; instead, it is retained in the unconscious. With the right triggers, whatever the emotions were, they will resurface. Sometimes the mechanism works to eliminate the entire memory from consciousness, sometimes just the feelings attached to the memory.

Olivia's father physically abused her. While she had full recall of many of the incidents, she could not recall her emotional experience attached to the memories. Yet the emotions remained housed in her unconscious. She had frequent, terrifying dreams about being stalked by a large man. By exploring her dream in the context of her childhood experience, we discovered that her stalker represented her father and the ongoing fear of him she unknowingly carried. By blocking the fear, she also successfully avoided the shame she experienced having interpreted her father's behavior as the result of her "badness." Once she reconnected with the feelings, she began to heal.

"Split-off numbing" creates a separate compartment for feelings and memories, giving you access to both but only one at a time. Even though you witness what's happening to you, it seems like watching a movie and not recognizing that you are the star. For instance, often when little children are sexually abused, they will fixate on something else, like the music playing in the background or a make-believe fantasy. This helps them leave their bodies while they're being molested and avoid the experience of what's happening. Later on, in adulthood, while having sex with a loving partner, the abused might be constantly distracted and unable to enjoy the intimacy or might have flashbacks of intense emotion from the abuse.

DENIAL

Guarding emotional pain with denial is similar to pretending, but it occurs on a much more unconscious level. Denial helps create a more tolerable reality if the true reality is too painful. With denial, you might convince yourself that what happened didn't happen or that it didn't happen the way you think it did. You might deny something about yourself. For instance, you might live as a social isolate to avoid fears of intimacy if this is the only way you have to minimize emotional pain. You may not see yourself as having fears of intimacy because staying isolated keeps intact your denial about it. We can be in denial of behavior or of our inner qualities.

Denial serves as a habitual way of responding so that you don't even recognize you have any pain. While denial allows you to avoid experiencing shame or other painful realities, it also restricts your awareness of your feelings and needs. It may work to keep your pain out of your conscious reach, but your behavior will often reflect it lurking in the shadows. For instance, people who've become adept at denial tend to be more likely to engage in serious self-destructive behavior. Because denial isn't fool-proof, people who use it also often suffer from addictions.

Denial differs from lying. Lying is a conscious behavior aimed to achieve a certain goal, whereas denial is unconscious. When lying, you actually know the truth. With denial, you convinced yourself of something else so that you no longer know what's true. It's hard to spot denial in yourself because of its ability to deceive you. Usually, others spot it for you.

PROJECTION

Projection is a bit more complicated. With projection, you unconsciously place your own feelings and needs onto someone else so you no longer experience them as originating from you.

A common projection of the sensitive-hearted is the belief that others don't like them, long before they have any information to warrant this belief. Since they have trouble liking themselves, they assume others won't like them either. With projection, though, the self-devaluation remains camouflaged and unconscious so that the only focus is on how someone else perceives you. As you can see, this guard isn't very protective at all. It still feels lousy to believe others don't like you, and the feeling can breed its own shame.

What's particularly unsettling about projection is that you may end up creating the very experience you projected, even though it really wasn't true to begin with. Mary was convinced that her husband was chronically angry with her. Every time he expressed the slightest disappointment, she perceived him angry. She interrogated him so incessantly that eventually he did get angry—not for the reasons she thought, but because she didn't believe him.

Once we understood Mary's fear of her own anger—she thought she was a bad person for being angry—she saw that she was the one who was angry, at her husband. Since she was prone to projecting, whenever she thought someone was angry with her, she first needed to learn to ask herself whether in fact she was angry with them.

BLAMING

Blaming is another way to help guard against pain. The mechanism works like this. If I judge my own needs and feelings, and I can find some way to make them your fault when they arise, then I don't have to be accountable for them. Essentially, I am a victim to my feelings or needs since I can make you the cause of them. The classic phrase people use to signify that blame is operative is "You made me feel this way." While this process may reduce the chances of feeling pain, this does not happen without a tremendous price. You will never be able to feel empowered or in command of your own self. If you blame others for your feelings or behavior, you are forever a victim to other people, and you won't be able to take credit for your own happiness either.

FEELING/NEED REPLACEMENT

With feeling/need replacement, you recognize your feelings as your own, but if they produce self-attack or judgment, you alter them into something. For instance, if you're fairly comfortable with anger but have little or no tolerance for sadness or fear, you may unconsciously shift all sadness and fear into anger. Here's an example. A couple is about to celebrate their first wedding anniversary. The husband tells his wife he is planning a very special night and wants to surprise her. He asks her to please be home by six o'clock at the latest. He hasn't told her, but he's having a present delivered to the house. It's not his usual style to give people surprises because he believes that others won't really like anything he has to offer. This time, however, he's convinced that his wife will really like the present, and he has grown very excited by the anticipation of pleasing her.

Six o'clock arrives and he receives a phone call from his wife. She apologizes and says her boss just informed her of a deadline at work that she must meet or her job is in jeopardy. Immediately upon hearing this, he becomes angry and tells her to stay as long as she wants because who really cares about anniversaries anyway.

In this scenario the husband had replaced his disappointment and hurt with anger because his true feelings leave him more vulnerable. Anger provides a safety net. He gets an outlet for a feeling, except they're not his real feelings. Can you think of any examples in your own life where you may have expressed a feeling that in hindsight you recognized was but a mask for another feeling?

INTELLECTUALIZATION

This is the process of converting feelings into thoughts. Feelings and needs, if they were disapproved of or shamed, get disconnected from oneself via staying focused on what one is thinking instead. Again, this occurs unconsciously and becomes a habitual mode of experiencing oneself. The "intellectualizer" may talk about feelings but without any real sensory experience of them. The descriptions remain on a cognitive level.

Usually when one feels something, there are accompanying sensations in the body. For instance, anger often brings on such physical sensations as rising body temperature, accelerated heartbeat, and/or a tensing of muscles. Fear may create sensations of butterflies in the stomach, lightheadedness, shallow breathing, and/or shakiness. For intellectualizers, however, these sensations are virtually nonexistent.

To check whether you use this mechanism, see how you answer the question "How do you feel about that?" If you often answer this with more than one or two words, you're probably describing thoughts rather than feelings.

Feelings are fairly basic. If you lose all the fancy words we have for them, you'll discover the four: mad, glad, sad, and afraid.

GRANDIOSITY

Grandiosity is the opposite experience of self-doubt, devaluation, inadequacy, shame, or unworthiness. It's the experience of greatness, super-humanness, limitlessness, and power. Often it is expressed in feelings of superiority and contempt for others. It provides an illusion of self-worth, but it's not the same as healthy self-esteem. It's different from healthy pride.

All of us have areas where we shine above others, and we deserve to feel really good about those areas. However, we also have limitations and areas where we may fall short of others. A healthy self-image allows us to be okay with our shortcomings. The grandiose defense, however, aims to block the unbearable shame of being less than the best at everything.

COMPENSATORY ENTITLEMENT

Entitlement is a necessary component of healthy self-esteem. It provides the inner sense that we deserve the things we desire. It's pretty cool, except when it becomes excessive. When entitlement runs amok, it exploits others and is toxic to relationships. While it aims to compensate for pain in the sensitive-hearted, it actually keeps the wounds alive because it is against our nature to truly feel good about ourselves if we are alienating or harming others intentionally.

"Compensatory entitlement" pressures you to take more than your fair share without regard for the rights of others. This mechanism is particularly resistant to change; it really keeps "bad self feelings" out of conscious reach. However, the cost to the quality of intimacy is enormous. You cannot possibly be intimate with someone if you view your own needs and rights as more important that those of others.

I'm not saying you should place your needs behind those of others. Quite the contrary: your own needs should be of utmost concern to you. But others deserve to have theirs attended to as well.

Remember John, who flew into a rage whenever he had to stand in line? Because he felt so cheated out of need fulfillment as a child, at the same time believing he was unworthy of fulfillment, he developed "compensatory entitlement" behavior. Until he recognized this, he would commonly walk up behind someone in line at the market and ask if he could go ahead. He didn't even notice that this was an unreasonable request. The person in front also had just as few items and was just as entitled to service as John was.

It wasn't as though there were extenuating circumstances, like needing to get medicine for a sick child. John simply believed the world should offer immediate fulfillment of his needs. Amazingly, he had a knack for finding people who indulged him, ultimately reinforcing his belief in his superiority.

One useful way to look at your own level of entitlement is to consider how much of your share of things you're comfortable and familiar with taking. If you experience less than your rightful share of things, you might be more drawn to people who take more than their fair share.

In relationships, the full 100 percent will be taken, but what portion do you allow yourself? If you value yourself, you should expect and receive an overall 50 percent. If you've created relationships where you consistently expect and take less than your share, you need to work on reclaiming what you've been giving away. If you've created relationships where you expect and receive more than your fair share, then you'll need to work on taking less. In either scenario, self-doubt creates the inequities. Working through that doubt will help to balance things out and keep you on the path toward thriving. You deserve your fair share: no more, no less.

I hope the above descriptions and examples have given you greater awareness of your own hidden pain, how you may have protected yourself from it, and some ways to heal it. If you are more the "wear my pain on my sleeve" type, then you probably already recognize how much self-doubt or devaluation can interfere with having a self-accepting existence. You already know that anything is better than swimming in a pool of unhealed pain.

However, it you're skeptical about the existence of your pain, you may be more reluctant to really see how it may be holding you back. Maybe your guards have worked pretty well. That's okay. Just try to take from this anything that relates to your experience.

Chapter Eight

Step Four: Lighten Your Load

Now you know how you were wounded and how it affected your sense of self-value. It's time to lighten your load and get rid of the unnecessary dead weight from unhealed pain and your guards against it.

Your self-image resembles a house. If built on a shaky foundation (like an earthquake fault), it won't be very sturdy. While some painting and redecorating may improve its appearance, no amount of cosmetic change will repair the underlying problems with the foundation.

You need to start instead where the structural damage lies and rebuild from there. That's not to say you have to throw away all the materials. Much will remain usable. But whatever is precious to keep will stand out far better if it's framed properly. You've got to get rid of whatever weakens the foundation.

PAIN BUSTERS

Healing emotional pain can seem like a never-ending process. Because we don't have the capacity as children to make conscious decisions about what we absorb from our surroundings, we're stuck taking it all in. We can't say to our parents or other important influences, "Hey, I don't like the way you're treating me. Until you treat me more kindly, I won't listen to you." As children, remember, we rely on adults to care for us. We internalize things much like a sponge absorbs water. It's not until much later that we develop psychological boundaries enabling us to reject that which seems unfriendly to our psyches. Unfortunately, though, for most of us, a whole bunch of unwanted stuff will be internalized before we reach the age and developmental maturity to set effective boundaries. Don't fret too much. This may sound hopeless, but it's not. You can rid yourself of unwanted cargo. But you must be willing to change your attitudes and actions by practicing the following five steps.

STEP ONE

Make a vow to pay close attention to the messages you've internalized that keep you from thriving. Every day, invite yourself to fully witness how you criticize, judge, shame, devalue, or talk down to yourself. While initially you may feel overwhelmed by just how much and how often you berate yourself (or use pain guards), you've got to commit to no more hiding.

STEP TWO

Transform your self-critical process into self-love. Whenever you say or do anything that diminishes your value, quickly make a statement of repair and then reframe. For instance, if you witness yourself using words like "stupid" or "idiot" when you make mistakes, apologize and create a positive replacement. You might say something like, "Oh, I made a mistake. I guess I didn't have the information I needed. What a great learning experience!" Or if you routinely make the same mistakes, get curious about why and leave judgment out. "Wow, I seem to hit the same wall over and over. I wonder what's going on with me. I'm sure there's a good reason I'm having trouble." Offer curiosity, not judgment.

STEP THREE

Practice giving yourself what you didn't get as a child. Use daily affirmations. Say things to yourself that you longed to hear, but didn't, from the people who cared for you as a child.

Of course, it would have been better to hear these things from your caregivers. Even though you can't turn back the clock and get what you missed out on, it's never too late to give to yourself what you need. Don't just say nice things. Do the things for yourself that others who cared for you didn't do for you. Practice praise, nurturing, and positive reinforcement. Forgive yourself for making mistakes. You might be thinking that it's not the same if you have to give this stuff to yourself. I agree. It's not the same. But that doesn't mean it isn't just as good. It might even be better, since you remain in charge.

STEP FOUR

Stop treating yourself like a rat in a laboratory experiment. You deserve better than that. If you're prone to rewarding yourself only when you achieve a goal or desired result, try giving yourself what you desire, regardless of whether you achieve your goals. Make rewards more immediate by breaking down tasks into small steps. Make sure you can actually achieve your goals. Don't set up yourself to fail. Let's say you decided that you couldn't go to the movies with your friends until you finished your laundry. Instead of making your pleasure contingent on whether you complete the task, go to the movies just because you want to go or complete a portion of your goal and then go.

If you find yourself repeatedly avoiding adult responsibilities or putting off necessary tasks, then don't go to the movies. Instead, try getting to the root of why you keep avoiding your duties. Don't try to bribe yourself into actions you're resisting. Rather, do a gentle and kind exploration of why you're resisting, then challenge yourself to try something different. You can always return to avoidant behavior if you need to, but why not try something else? The message here is to put to rest your military style and replace it with love and encouragement.

STEP FIVE

Stop criticizing your being. Criticizing anything about your essence is particularly self-destructive because there's nothing you can do about it. If you are big-boned, for instance, and you're critical of this, you're destined for misery. While we can certainly change many things like attitudes and behaviors, we cannot change our basic nature. Sure, advancements in technology enable us to change physical attributes, even alter our genetic predisposition to disease. But if you pursue any of these avenues to change who you are, make sure you're not coming out of a place of self-hatred.

NEUTRALIZING A HARSH INNER CRITIC

Just like humility and self-consciousness help the survival of our species, so, too, does a little bit of self-criticism. We carry the capacity to be critical in order to evaluate situations for possible danger. We learn that crossing the street against a red light is dangerous. Were it not for our ability to distinguish a good move from a bad one in this sense, we'd be in big trouble. Beyond a strict survival sense, being critical also gives us the capacity to determine what we like and don't like. That enhances our ability to find pleasure and to experience enjoyable feelings. Oftentimes, however, the capacity to be critical can become excessive and demeaning to the self and/or others.

If your inner critic makes you feel bad or if it keeps you from creating warm, intimate relationships, then you're no longer using your capacity in a self-adaptive way. It's become too harsh and is no longer effective. Neutralizing a harsh inner critic happens in four steps: naming the criticism; identifying from whom it really originated; giving the criticism back to whomever delivered it in the first place; and deciding whether there is anything constructive about the criticism that you may want to keep.

STEP ONE

Make a list of all the things about yourself you tend to be critical of. Be as inclusive as you can.

STEP TWO

Next to each item, see if you can recall from where the criticism originated and how old you were at the time. If you believe that you were the sole creator of the criticism, see if you can identify whether a significant caregiver may have said anything similar to you and who it was.

STEP THREE

Once you've identified from whom the criticisms originated, create an imaginary conversation with the person you identified. Give the criticism back.

STEP FOUR

Determine whether the criticism actually has merit. Sometimes criticisms have merits that can only be seen once the shaming aspects are removed. Shame or its relatives (feelings of inadequacy, low self-esteem, self-devaluation) will prohibit your ability to see the value in a criticism because it hurts too much.

Peter became quickly ashamed any time he laughed in uproarious delight. In his head he heard (no, he wasn't hearing voices), "Be quiet, or everyone will think you're an idiot. You laugh like a snorting pig." Ouch. Peter believed that he had actually come up with this assessment of his laugh on his own. While it's true that he formulated the specifics of his attack on himself, the makings of it traced back to an early wound.

When we explored Peter's criticism of his laugh, we discovered that his mother used to tease him as a little boy whenever he would let out a good belly laugh. In fact, he recalled that she even called him a pig. While his mother meant it in good humor, Peter was only five, and he experienced her as making fun of him. Once when they had gone to the zoo together, his mother had expressed disgust of the pigs. She said she hated how they smelled. Peter unknowingly linked his mother's comment about the pigs to her comment about his laugh. He felt small in her eyes and believed she thought he was a disgusting pig. This got lodged into his unconscious and, as an adult, served to inhibit his experience of joy whenever he felt like laughing.

Using the steps outlined above, Peter identified the criticism and from where it actually originated. In order to neutralize it, we did an imagery exercise where he envisioned himself standing in front of his mother and holding the hand of his five-year-old.

Looking into her eyes, he said, "Mother, I felt very hurt when you called me a pig when I laughed. Whether you meant to hurt me or not, I must acknowledge that I became ashamed of my laugh and now I continue to criticize myself. I don't want to continue doing that. I'm giving back your comment to you. I no longer have any use for it. You can take it back or dump it. But I will no longer wear it."

Once Peter was able to metaphorically give back the criticism from his mother, he was able to look at his laugh with greater objectivity and decide for himself whether he was fine with it. He concluded that he liked his laugh and didn't see any need to change it.

Alexa offers us an example of actually finding merit in the criticism. Alexa's mother never liked her style of dress. On many occasions, her mother voiced this to her in a rather harsh and demeaning way. Over the years, Alexa found herself actually picking clothes that she knew her mother wouldn't like. She never checked in with herself about whether she liked them; she just picked the opposite of her mother's taste.

As an adult, she really had no idea what she liked wearing. But once she was able to let go of the criticism, she had room to evaluate her wardrobe without shaming herself or hearing her mother's criticism. She discovered that she had been picking clothes that really didn't suit her own style. She was then free to pick out what she liked to wear whether her mother liked it or not, rather than to spite her mother.

In doing this exercise, you'll probably notice that you've added your own details to many of the criticisms you internalized from others. Don't worry if you can't identify the source. It's most important to just note how the process is alive today. Often there won't even be a clear-cut source. Sometimes we internalize messages from society at large or from things we see or read in the media. Or it may be that your caregivers didn't say harsh or critical things directly to you, but they still displayed a general attitude of contempt toward you or role-modeled excessive criticism. In essence, you may have learned excessive criticism by example rather than by direct assault on you.

THE TREASURE HUNT

Once you've busted the pain and harsh internalized critic, you're free to find the hidden treasures that resulted from your life's experiences. Hopefully you're already beginning to see how amazing you are. Your wounds are gifts, no matter how big or small. They're part of who you are. This exercise will help you strengthen your belief in your true value.

Make a list of your top ten memories from when you felt wounded. (If you were badly abused as a child, you probably have a lot more. You don't need to limit yourself to only ten.) Remember not to judge whether you should feel wounded. For each wound on the list, write an apology letter to yourself. Make it come from the person or institution who hurt you.

The letter may look something like this. Modify it to fit the specifics of your pain.

Dear (your name),

I'm so terribly sorry for having hurt your feelings in the way that I did when I (name the event). I know that you have suffered deeply as a result. You are not responsible for my behavior. Please don't hold yourself accountable in any way. If I could take back what I said or did that hurt you, I would. While I can't do that, I can take ownership of it now and free you to heal. (Sign the letter as though it came from the wounding source.)

After you do the letter, go back and identify something you gained from the original experience you felt wounded by. How did it strengthen you? What preparation did it give you to handle things in life that you otherwise would not have gotten? You can transform your pain into a treasure.

Sally endured many losses and deep feelings of abandonment. She can now look back on her childhood, recognizing the strength it gave her to handle life's difficult moments. She developed more patience and understanding than most other people who had never experienced what she had. Once she healed her pain, she was able to use what happened to her to better empathize with others. She was able to see the complexities of relationships.

Her childhood experiences, while unhappy, forced her to examine her behavior. They inspired her to make constructive changes. She was more tolerant and less judgmental of other people's idiosyncratic responses to life. She developed a more loving model of parenting that she hopes to use with the children she plans to have someday.

Once you've identified your resources, place them in a treasure chest to be cherished and valued. Write yourself friendly reminders of your value and inner gifts, and read them every day.

Chapter Nine

Step Five: Recognize How Unhealed Wounds Have Harmed Your Adult Relationships

Past pain is hard to conquer. If only that were the last step toward well-being. Unfortunately, you must also face the fallout of this pain in terms of how it affects your adult relationships. Old wounds, when left unhealed, not only create a sensitive heart but will also wreak havoc with your present relationships.

Our wounds want to find a place to heal. If we are not consciously taking the time and energy to put them to rest, our wounds will direct our behavior to re-create situations similar to the original wounding experience. You will unknowingly attract people and events into your life that are similar to the original wounding experiences—unconsciously, you are hoping for a better outcome this time.

Wounding events have a ripple effect on our entire lives. The less opportunity there was for healing, the more they're likely to harm our relationships later on.

In many ways, our tendency toward this re-creation can be a highly positive force. It works beautifully if your childhood experiences brought you an inner sense of peace, comfort, and tranquility. Then you would be set up to re-create situations resembling that climate. But since you're reading this book, I'll assume that wasn't your dominant experience. So you have work to do to change the natural course.

The re-creation can happen with your friends, colleagues, coworkers, employers, lovers, or children. It's not a conscious process. In fact, once you're aware of your wounds, you'll probably be consciously attempting to avoid relationships where you will be hurt again.

You'll date the guy you think is the opposite of your father who beat you. You'll work for someone who seems gentle and encouraging, unlike your mother, who criticized everything you did. You'll seek friends who appear giving and caring, unlike the kids in your school, who were only nice to you when they needed something from you.

There's one big problem, however. While you try to create something different, your wounds create blind spots that keep you from seeing how your behavior sabotages what you desire. Or you don't notice the red flags waved by those you attract that scream for your attention. Noticing old wounds just isn't enough. You have to heal them and actually change their course.

Take Sally, for example. She entered adulthood aware that she had been deeply wounded, but she assumed that time would heal her wounds. While she had made a conscious decision never to tolerate unhealthy relationships, she continued to pick guys who exploited her and failed to treat her with the respect she deserved. When she picked Bob, her latest boyfriend, before coming to therapy, she thought he was a good guy. But he was no less disrespectful to her—it just came in a different form.

Bob told her she was boring and "high maintenance." He constantly broke promises and showed up hours late for their dates, always with some lame excuse. He even called her fat during arguments to exploit her already shattered body image.

Remember Tom, whose mother threatened to send him to boarding school whenever he failed to follow her directions? Tom learned to protect himself from his fear of abandonment by always expecting the worst. He actually found it comforting to fear the worst. Then, if something better happened, he considered it a bonus. But once he became an adult, without dealing with the fear and its original source, this wound actually directed him toward the very things he feared.

At his job, he worried he'd be fired if he made a mistake. Sure enough, he made mistakes and his boss fired him. The tragedy for Tom was that he believed he was fired for his mistakes. But his boss thought his work excellent, even though it wasn't perfect.

In actuality, Tom's attitude reflected such pessimism that his coworkers couldn't stand him and wouldn't work cooperatively with him. While Tom's boss liked Tom's work, he wasn't willing to jeopardize his other employees' work environment. That's why he fired Tom.

Remember Betty, whose father constantly criticized her appearance? Her mother never stood up for her. She went so far as to put Betty on diets to prevent her from "upsetting her father."

Betty wasn't even remotely overweight. (Not that her parents' approach would have been any better if she had been.) Her father simply needed someone to criticize because he hadn't healed his own childhood wounds. Betty learned to hate her body, mistrust men, and fear intimacy.

In case you don't recall, Betty married a guy who had an affair, told her it was her fault, and then left her with their two children. When Betty met her husband, he seemed quite the opposite of her father. He told her she was beautiful, he rarely drank, and he seemed kind-hearted.

But Betty couldn't trust him because she didn't view herself as beautiful. And because she had internalized her father's treatment of her, she didn't believe anyone could truly love her.

Now, while better than most of the guys Betty had relationships with, Betty's husband wasn't a winner. In fact, he was far less sincere than he portrayed himself to be. He actually had a lot of issues about commitment. Betty needed to discover how she had created a no-win situation for herself and how she was likely to sabotage future relationships if she didn't grow to value and appreciate herself.

While Betty wanted to believe her husband thought she was beautiful, she consistently rejected his compliments. Unfortunately, her husband didn't have the capacity to understand this dynamic. He eventually lost interest in trying to convince her. In fact, after so much rejection, he even stopped viewing Betty as attractive and found her negativity unappealing.

He'd tried so many times to compliment her, and each time she persisted in attacking herself. Ultimately, he gave up. Granted, Betty was not responsible for his decision to have an affair, but she did need to look at how she interrupted any possibility of feeling good about herself.

HOW WE SABOTAGE

The havoc of an unhealed heart can show up in a variety of ways. Sometimes, as in Tom's situation, it manifests as a self-fulfilling prophecy, where he feared something would happen and unknowingly created the very thing he feared.

Sometimes it comes in the form of negating your right to a need and thereby not allowing it to be fulfilled. This is especially tragic when a relationship would actually provide that which you yearn for, but you are afraid to let it in.

Self-sabotage is a direct result of not feeling deserving of whatever it is you desire. Let's say your husband comes to hug you after a long day of work, happy to see you and eager to reconnect. You crave affection, but you believe you haven't earned it. You believe you're not worthy of his love because you didn't accomplish all the things you were supposed to do that day. He could care less, but you push him away and busy yourself doing the dishes in order to feel more worthy. This is not a case of somebody else depriving you of what you desire.

Rather, it's a case of the "Do I/Don't I Deserve It" Dance having defeated you—where you provide the obstacles to satisfaction.

Another way of sabotaging is by expecting others to know what you need or want without asking for it. In an ideal world, your significant caregivers would have been masterful at predicting and adequately responding to all of your needs. Then you would have a sense of fullness and would carry a well of security and trust.

This is not the case for most of us, even if our parents truly had their hearts in the right place. Because of the imperfections and the resulting wounds, shame has the fertile soil in which to grow. The shame creates a negating of certain needs, which then perpetuates dysfunctional ways of communicating them. It's reasonable to expect someone to give you what you ask for if they know what it is and agree to provide it. It's not reasonable to expect others to read your mind.

We also sabotage by having unrealistic expectations of what relationships can actually provide. Adult relationships cannot repair the damage from childhood. While our sensitive hearts seek soothing from others, ultimately it's up to our own selves to repair the damage. Even if you happen to find other adults who are willing to parent you all over again, you will still end up disappointed. They won't be able to do it well enough either. And you can't have a mutually loving and supportive adult relationship when your partner takes on the role of parent.

While it's tempting to search for people to give us the things we were deprived of in childhood, no one can replace what wasn't there. Healthy relationships, however, can promote growth and facilitate healing. They can make it easier for you to do your healing. But they cannot do the healing for you.

IGNORING RED FLAGS

With some people, it will not be worth your time and energy to cultivate a relationship of any substance. They may be fine individuals for certain people, but for you they are bad news. When we have sensitive spots from childhood wounds, there will be certain behaviors and attitudes in others that will feel particularly sore, at least while we are doing the healing.

Picking people for social or intimate relationships who clearly demonstrate an unwillingness or inability to meet your needs is another likely way that unhealed wounds can harm relationships. This is especially destructive when your expectations are unreasonable. This would be like going to a hardware store for your groceries. At best, you may be able to find some candy at the checkout stand, but you certainly won't be able to get the necessary supplies you came for.

You may have noticed that you have a strong negative reaction to certain things that people do, while also noticing that these same things don't particularly bother others around you. These should stand out as red flags for you. That doesn't mean, necessarily, that you should avoid all relationships with people who push your buttons. Actually, this kind of triggering can sometimes serve as a catalyst for working on your issues. Sometimes, though, the wound is still too raw, and some behaviors are toxic. These should probably be avoided. Let me give you a few examples.

Remember Jane, who became the target of a nasty custody battle during her parents' divorce? For years she lived surrounded with tremendous conflict and hostility. Her mother constantly made derogatory comments about her father. Her father ranted and raved about how hysterical and ungrateful her mother was. Jane had no one to turn to. She was so frightened of losing her parents that she developed whatever peacemaking skills she could to ward off the possibility of the loss she feared.

This was far too heavy a burden for a child, yet as a strong-willed girl, Jane would not give up.

As an adult, Jane unconsciously sought out relationships with people who filled their lives with high conflict and drama. She was so familiar with the role of soother and problem-solver that she couldn't help but get involved with people she thought needed rescuing. Jane would become resentful and get tired of her friends for constantly using her for help with their problems. These kinds of relationships were not conducive to healing the wounds from her parents' divorce.

Later, after doing a good deal of healing, learning how to set better boundaries, and managing to refrain from diving in to rescue those around her, Jane opted out of some of these connections. She left her job as an executive assistant to the man famous for screaming at his subordinates. Since he wasn't willing to change, she came to recognize that there was no point in staying.

But there were a few people in her life who were willing to recognize and improve their dysfunctional behavior. They changed their relationships with her to a more peaceful level of relating, and she was able to keep these people as friends. (You'll learn more about setting boundaries in Chapter 14.)

If you suffered physical abuse as a child, a number of behaviors are likely to trigger too much stuff. Though not experienced by everyone as abusive, they will seem abusive to you and might ultimately be destructive to your healing. For instance, people who like to play around physically by jokingly slapping your face (lightly, of course), or people who like to wrestle, or those who have loud and animated voices especially when angry may frighten you too much.

You won't be able to convince yourself emotionally that you're not in any danger even though you may know this intellectually. Yet, because of the propensity to re-create that which is familiar, if you have unhealed wounds surrounding your abuse, you might be attracted to these kind of people. Against your better rational judgment, you may be prone to developing relationships with them, anyway.

Remain extra cautious before deciding whether these people truly won't harm you or whether they in fact exhibit tendencies toward actual violence. If your wounds were less overt, you'll need to more closely examine the links between what pushes your buttons as an adult and what created your childhood hurts.

IDENTIFYING WITH THE AGGRESSOR

Tragically, you might harm your adult relationships by treating others in the same ways that harmed or wounded you. I doubt that you would do this consciously or with malicious intent. But remember, any time you feel you've been victimized, and yes children often qualify as true victims, you run the risk of potentially violating, exploiting, or even abusing others. This usually happens because you are still entrenched in bruised-heart mentality and believe you're acting defensively for your own protection and survival rather than offensively to harm.

Some of you may have developed a hardened edge. You may not even be aware that you treat others harshly or without regard for their rights. You may feel justified in your behavior because you really don't see how it resembles the bad treatment you received. Or you may mislabel certain behaviors of others as objectively harmful because you don't recognize that you have options as an adult that you didn't have as a child.

Remember Susan, who coped with her mother's excessive criticism by becoming a meticulous housekeeper? She developed other behaviors that interfered with her relationships. She became so reactive to criticism that even when it was delivered to her in an appropriate and constructive way, she reacted as though she were being attacked. When her boss once told her she needed to improve on some of her job-related tasks, she believed him to be controlling and harsh.

One day she quit abruptly without giving any notice because she thought he was an unbearable bully. With hindsight, Susan was able to realize that her supervisor had every right to comment on her work performance. He was just doing his job. He even spoke to her in a gentle tone and often had praised her many talents.

Unfortunately for Susan, she only focused on what he wasn't happy with. The manner in which she quit might have been appropriate had she really had a hostile, critical, exploitative boss. But in this context it was Susan's reaction that had the quality of harshness, not her boss's.

One of the worst ways in which unhealed wounds wreak havoc is when you treat your own self in the way you were originally wounded; in other words, when you identify with the aggressor and behave unkindly to yourself. This actually sets up others to treat you in the same manner.

Jane constantly criticized her body. She hated her shape and size, and she continually dated guys who criticized and rejected her. Don, whose mother constantly invaded his privacy, distanced himself from relationships. While he longed for social connection, he kept finding himself attracting intrusive and invasive people. He had no idea why. He eventually isolated himself to the degree that he had no friends and no social life whatsoever.

Candace, who was the victim of sexual abuse, treated herself with no respect for her body. She hung out in bars and if a guy paid any attention to her, she felt compelled to have sex with him, and not because of her own desire. Rather, she disregarded her own needs and believed she had to service others. It's not surprising that she found many men willing to treat her with the same disregard.

Adam, whose father ridiculed him for every mistake, identified with his father's perception of him. In adulthood, he expected that others would not find any value in his opinions. He expected to be seen as wrong and stupid. Sure enough, he encountered many people who treated him as though he were stupid. He found people who had a dominant need to always be right (no doubt a symptom of their own unhealed wounds). They were more than happy to allow Adam to claim responsibility for any misunderstandings or mishaps.

IDENTIFYING HOW YOU'VE HARMED YOUR RELATIONSHIPS

Take some time to truly assess the behaviors and dynamics that may have sabotaged your relationships or kept them in a state of distress. Answer the following questions.

1. Do you do any of the following compulsively: shopping, spending money, using drugs or alcohol to excess, working, gambling, cleaning, exercising, or eating?
2. Can you accept positive input when it's offered to you, or do you tend to downplay or reject the input?
3. Do you expect others to repair wounds from your past or to act like the parent you never had?
4. Do you let other people make decisions for you, and, if so, do you later resent them?
5. Do you censor your own opinions and expect others to pull them out of you?
6. Are you impatient, irritable, or hostile toward others before you have even had any interaction with them?
7. Do you bend over backward to keep people happy?
8. Do you avoid any kind of confrontation?

Answering these questions should help you better recognize how you may be harming your relationships. In doing so, you've paved the way for accepting the past and your part in re-creating it. You've opened the door to accept full self-responsibility as a healthy, happy Thriver.

Chapter Ten

Step Six: Accept the Past and Your Part in Re-Creating It

I cannot emphasize strongly enough that in order to heal, you must let go of any remnants of self-blame or responsibility for the things that happened to you as a child that you could not control. You also must accept responsibility for events in your adulthood where you did or do have control. Otherwise you will remain trapped in a vicious cycle of re-creating your old wounds over and over and perpetually feeling victimized throughout your life.

The tricky part, though, is to know the difference. Unfortunately, when wounds go unhealed, whether above or beneath the surface, it's often very difficult to distinguish what you have control over, and hence what you are accountable for, from what doesn't belong to you.

When approaching this stage of healing, I discourage you from using words like "blame" or "fault." They create strong negative connotations for most of us, thus only serving to induce shame or heighten any preexisting shame. As you've learned, this kind of shame doesn't promote healing; it prohibits or disrupts healing. Instead, I encourage you to focus on words like awareness, choice, accountability, and responsibility.

You have not re-created your wounds intentionally. You're not masochistic. You don't intentionally set out to cause yourself distress. You cannot be responsible for something you've been in the dark about. But once you understand this process and the importance of leaving bruised- or sensitive-heart mentality behind, you no longer need to blame others. You can identify how you set yourself up for distress, and you can take charge of the things you need to change in order for you to stop re-creating it. You become ready for healthy-hearted, Thriver living.

This is not the legal system. Don't get caught up in the notion that you should be accountable for everything that's happened in your life since you became a legal adult at eighteen. You're not being judged for whether you should be tried as an adult or as a child. This isn't a courtroom. This is your life and your opportunity to live it with full awareness and conscious choice.

This is a process. Most likely, you will rediscover again and again how you repeat your own wounds. You'll make tons of mistakes. It's like learning a whole new language; you don't just hear it and speak it fluently. You have to hear the words, phrases, and intonations many, many times. Then, you need to repeat what you hear again and again.

There may also be times when you forget to practice and fall back into your own language. Learning and growth is ever more likely under conditions of acceptance and understanding of the process.

WHAT YOU ACTUALLY CAN CONTROL

Ultimately, all we really control is our own behavior. That includes our actions, feelings, perceptions, and thoughts. Those who have children or adults dependent on them for care also have a fair amount of control over them. Because children and other dependent individuals don't have the same choices as adults, even when it appears that they have options to choose from, their options remain far more limited and are confined to those provided by caregivers and other adults.

Relative to adults, children really don't have the same level of choice. Of course, as they grow older, they are usually offered more and more freedom to make their own decisions. Ideally, by the time we reach adulthood, we can fully realize our capacity to choose. Yet whether an adult actually recognizes his or her capacity to make choices depends a lot on whether old wounds remain operative.

For instance, you can't choose a healthy relationship with yourself (or anyone else for that matter) if you're still weighed down by unhealed stuff that's continuing to seek resolution. You can't choose a career if you still believe you have to be what your father or mother expects you to be. You can't choose what you want to eat if you believe you don't know what's good for you because your parents told you that you are incapable of caring for yourself. These unhealed wounds prohibit free choice. They keep you trapped in a dependent relationship in the world, similar to the way a child might be trapped.

A ten-year-old boy may choose not to go to his friend's house on Thursday after school because he knows that if he doesn't finish his homework, he may not get good grades. If he makes this choice because he himself desires good grades, then he'll be far less likely to feel cheated or wounded.

But if he makes the decision not to go because he fears that poor grades will lose him his dad's approval, he's really not making a choice. Because he needs his father's love and care, his choices become dependent on his father's influence. If he fears the person he relies on for care will harm him or possibly abandon him, he has to choose not to go to ensure his survival. You can see he hasn't really chosen at all.

An independent adult, on the other hand, would not fear these consequences but, instead, those imposed by his or her own conscience. Naturally, parents, other caregivers, and society must make choices for children, especially those a child isn't developmentally ready to make.

It wouldn't be appropriate, for instance, for a five-year-old to make choices about how to save money for college. Yet this might be quite appropriate for a sixteen-year-old. Hopefully, the choices that adults make for their children truly respect the needs of the child and attend to the child's level of maturity. Choices should not be made out of the adult's need for control.

Many would argue that adults don't really have free choice either. This argument does have good merit. Wherever we choose to live, there are laws to abide by and social mores that influence our decisions about how to behave. All actions have a potential consequence. And because of our conscience and morals, our choices will be somewhat driven by attention to factors outside ourselves.

The major difference between an independent adult and a dependent child is that children have to rely on adults for their care and survival. This becomes especially true the younger they are. They're stuck with what's offered to them. In adulthood, you don't have to depend on anyone else for your survival, and you can usually leave a situation if it doesn't suit you.

Unfortunately, most people who've been victimized don't see their options. They don't see that they can leave or change their circumstances. They don't recognize that they don't really need others for survival, including many of the things they needed as a child. At least they don't need these supplies from others.

As adults, they can now provide them for themselves. Often, however, they don't trust themselves enough to fulfill their own needs. They still experience themselves as needy and dependent on others. They still perceive themselves as controlled by the world around them.

In order to cope with your childhood, you may have developed the illusion of being in control of other people's behavior. As many of the examples show, children will go to great lengths to please those who provide their care. They'll accommodate, acquiesce, or change their behavior altogether if they believe it will help them get their needs met. Probably, the more abuse or neglect you experienced, the more likely you were to have developed the illusion that you could control other people's behavior.

You may have spent your whole lifetime trapped, trying to get others to behave in the ways you think you need them to because you don't yet know or trust that you can meet your needs yourself. You don't need approval, love, admiration, acceptance, validation, or confirmation from anyone other than yourself.

While you may prefer to have these from others, you don't actually need them met by others and certainly not from any one particular source. As soon as you accept that you have the ultimate control over providing for your own needs, you accept responsibility for yourself. You can also let go of the ideas that you are in control of anything other than yourself and that you are not responsible for other people. That doesn't mean your behavior doesn't have an impact on others.

If you are cruel to others and you hurt them, you are accountable for that. If you exploit your power over anyone who is truly vulnerable, like a child or incapacitated adult, you are responsible for your actions.

THE RESPONSIBILITY BOX

The first step in claiming your own responsibility for your choices is to clear the path of anything that gets in the way. As you've learned, the obstacles include shame (and its relatives) and the self-protective guards that compel you to claim stuff that really belongs to someone else or some other institution. You end up with too much on your plate and then not enough room to claim what's actually yours.

Kenny's father used to hit Kenny whenever he was in a bad mood. But rather than claim his bad mood and leave Kenny out of it, Kenny's father told him that he deserved to be spanked because Kenny didn't do what his father asked, like cleaning his room, drying the dishes, or making his bed. Kenny believed that he was responsible for his father's rage and that his father had no other choice but to spank him.

When I asked Kenny how he was disciplined, he said, "Oh, just the normal spankings. I caused a lot of trouble as a child and made my father so angry. No wonder he beat me."

What Kenny didn't realize is that he was just a kid. He could in no way be responsible for his father's behavior. His father was solely responsible for his bad temper and out-of-control behavior. His father blamed Kenny for his own misbehaviors. Kenny needed appropriate consequences, boundaries, and structure, not beatings. But since his father wouldn't claim responsibility for his own actions, Kenny took on the burden that he had control over his father's actions. If only he could keep from behaving in a way that angered his father, he wouldn't get beaten.

Kenny's father was repeating the generational cycle of dysfunction. His own father taught him that he caused other people's actions. He never learned that he was in control of his own behavior and not the behavior of others. By the time Kenny was an adult, he, too, was set up to re-create this pattern within his relationships.

Fortunately for Kenny's kids, Kenny came to realize that this pattern wasn't working well for him. He consistently felt out of control and ashamed of how he kept blaming his kids for things he intellectually recognized were not their fault. But he was stuck. He didn't know what he needed to do to become responsible for his own actions. He needed to learn something new.

Kenny eventually couldn't deal with himself anymore and came for therapy. Once we cleared out the shame, Kenny was able to take the next brave step. He denounced the illusion of responsibility for things he couldn't control and cleared the path to take ownership of that which belonged to him. He stopped yelling at his kids and apologized to them for his behavior.

When he found himself getting angry, he would say, "Hey, kids, Dad's a little irritable right now. Please go to your rooms if you feel like making a lot of noise, because I have to get my work done and I need quiet."

Now he doesn't blame his kids for his own level of frustration or difficulty coping with his feelings. He claims his own annoyance without creating shame in his kids.

To help release responsibility that doesn't belong to you, try the following exercise. First, make a list of everything you have carried responsibility for, from childhood through present, you believe doesn't belong to you. Remember, unless you were in a position of power over someone, like a child or dependent adult, you are not responsible for the actions, feelings, or thoughts of others.

That doesn't mean that you don't have an influence over other people. It means that, ultimately, other independent adults are responsible for themselves.

Now, for each item on your list, imagine putting the responsibility into a box, wrapping it, and mailing it back to the person or institution you believe wrongly dumped it on you. In some cases, if your earliest experiences led you to believe you were responsible for other people's behavior, you may take the blame automatically, even when no one directly gave it to you. You've then become a "habitual blame taker." While you may not have anyone in particular to give responsibility back to, you must still give it away. Try the image of a trash can or some other dumping ground. Kenny imagined the following letter along with the package.

"Dear Dad: Enclosed please find your bad temper and your words that I am the cause of it. You created your own bad moods and took them out on me. I did not deserve your treatment of me, and I especially did not deserve to

be held accountable for your behavior. Do what you want with it, but I'm not going to hold onto it anymore."

Though you won't actually be putting this "return gift" in the mail, the imagery of placing responsibility where it belongs will empower you.

After making your list of the places where you've taken too much responsibility, it's time to look back at your life as an adult. Do it without shaming or blaming yourself. Simply take inventory of the times in your life when you now realize you may have had responsibility, even though you didn't see it at the time.

For instance, Kenny recognized how he was repeating his father's pattern with his own children. There was nothing more healing for his children than to hear their father apologize. They were relieved of the burden of his responsibility and free to start becoming responsible for their own actions.

If it seems appropriate, I would highly recommend that you actually express your accountability directly to the people you believe you've burdened. It may be a little awkward if you are no longer in contact with them, but at the very least you might try writing a letter, even if you choose not to send it. You should not express yourself directly to the person if you believe it would harm the person in any way or if you believe you would be harmed.

For instance, let's say you had an affair twenty years ago that your ex-spouse never knew about. You've both moved on, and you believe it would only hurt him to hear about it now. In this case, just take full responsibility for your behavior in your own mind. You may have been justifying your actions for all these years, saying that you had every right to your affair because your ex-husband ignored your needs.

If you see what I'm talking about here, you'll understand that no one can make you have an affair. The choice of what to do with your loneliness is still yours. In this scenario, telling your ex about your transgressions would probably serve yourself while potentially harming your ex. If he never asked you about your fidelity, he might not want to know. He should be allowed this choice.

Even in situations where you may have been victimized as an adult, it's important to claim responsibility for any part you might have played—perhaps by perpetuating silence, or not sharing the experience with a trusted friend, or not seeking help.

Please do not hear this as "blaming" yourself. By now, I hope you understand this isn't at all what I mean. Remember, once you can fully see the choices you make, you will become empowered to make healthier and more life-affirming ones.

COMMITMENT TO SELF-RESPONSIBILITY

Recall Betty, whose father constantly criticized her body, calling her fat and ugly. As a child, she was clearly a victim to her father's mental and psychological mistreatment. She had nowhere else to go and needed his care. She could not physically leave.

But as an adult, Betty frequently dated guys who judged her body harshly. Because her wound remained unhealed, she didn't recognize that she had the power not to select these men. As an adult, she had to learn that she was responsible for how she treated her body and how she allowed others to treat her.

Make a commitment to stop treating yourself the way you've been wounded. The old way may be the most familiar, but it won't help you heal. You need to practice a new way. Eventually, it, too, will become what's most familiar. You must hold accountable those who wounded you in the past, but now you must develop conscious awareness of how you continue to keep those wounds alive. With this awareness, you'll be able to claim responsibility for what's truly yours to hold and be free to let go of the rest.

Chapter Eleven

Step Seven: Claim Your Healthy-Hearted Power

You've been working really hard and hopefully learning a lot. Now it's time to stop and smell the roses, or the coffee, or whatever tickles your fancy. More seriously, you truly must take a breather from all this work. You've been busy exploring, accepting, recognizing, healing, and changing. You must also make some room to play and enjoy yourself, as well as to rest. Healthy-hearted power requires a balance among work, rest, and play.

You've been discovering how you've been wounded, how you've coped with your sensitive heart, how you've protected yourself from further injury, and how you've inadvertently set up yourself to continue the wounding process. At this point you've also released at least some of your self-criticism and tendency toward self-devaluation, if not all of it.

You now know that you cannot reasonably expect yourself to stop the re-creation process without the necessary knowledge of how it functions and the tools to stop it. You've begun to recognize the value in accepting responsibility for your own process. You no longer need to wait for others to provide your healing. You can provide for yourself. You know that others serve as potential helpers to your growth process, but you also understand that ultimately you navigate your own well-being.

You've learned about what you have control over and what you don't, and that knowledge has given you the power to choose. You've also learned to cherish all of your experiences.

So now it's time to pat yourself on the back. Recognize your courage and your dedication. Celebrate! Do something really special for yourself. Don't wait for someone else to do it for you. You can do it for yourself.

One of the most beautiful moments in my practice was the day that a young woman I worked with decided to throw herself the party she always wanted but had never received as a child. Adrianne was raised in a religion that prohibited the celebration of birthdays. Because she didn't grow up with other children of her faith, she felt like an outcast. She wasn't allowed to go to birthday parties, and her own birthday was never acknowledged.

Adrianne's parents were acting in accordance with their faith. But they didn't recognize the embarrassment and alienation Adrianne experienced for being so different. She wanted more than anything to belong. Had Adrianne been among other children of the same faith, it may not have bothered her as much. That's something we'll never know. What Adrianne did know was that she felt deprived and cheated.

As an adult, Adrianne longed for a birthday party. Yet she never really felt entitled to one. She thought that the only way she could ever have one would be if someone else would throw it for her. She waited many years—but the party never happened.

In her therapy, Adrianne recognized that she no longer needed to wait for someone else to have a party for her. She discovered that she could give herself the party she longed for. For her twenty-eighth birthday, she decided to have the party she never had as a child.

Rather than celebrate as an adult, she decided to throw herself the party she wished she'd had as a child. She chose the age at which she had felt most deprived and created a party suitable for a ten-year-old.

Adrianne told her friends to bring along their favorite games from childhood. She decorated with things that would intrigue a child of ten and scattered lots of balloons and candy bowls about her apartment.

She bought ice cream and the cake she'd always dreamed of. She hired a magician. Some of her girlfriends even slept over to enjoy an all-night gigglefest. She also got an unexpected bonus. Not only did she please her own sensitive self, she also pleased her friends immensely.

In your own way, do something special for yourself to honor what you feel you lost from your childhood. Be creative. Buy or make yourself a toy you never had. If you have a child or are close to one, like a niece or nephew, take the child on a full-day outing of sheer pleasure, with no agenda.

Have ice cream before lunch, forget homework for a day, make up silly rhymes, feed the ducks, fly a kite, toss a ball around with no goal, or do jumping jacks while singing nursery rhymes. It doesn't really matter what you do, just do something you wouldn't ordinarily allow yourself.

Set aside at least fifteen minutes of every workday to appreciate something about yourself. Draw a picture to celebrate your creativity, call a friend to celebrate your desire for connection, make a pie to celebrate your culinary aptitude, light scented candles to stimulate olfactory pleasure.

You're a living, breathing, sensing, feeling, thinking, spiritual being. Invite the whole of you to join in.

On your days off work, create more time for play and to enjoy your life. If you've overfilled your life with "have-to-dos" and "must-dos," it's time to reassess your priorities. It may be a slow process to reorganize your life to include playtime, but there's no better time than the present to set that in motion. Schedule it into your calendar if you must.

Make an appointment with yourself for playtime. If you find yourself resisting, examine that impulse. You're the one in charge. If you won't make the time for yourself, at least own that as your choice.

If you've tended to avoid responsibilities, make a list of goals you wish to accomplish. Begin by setting those in motion. Once you're feeling better about yourself, you'll often find an increase in energy to motivate you toward action. You still need playtime, but you might want to negotiate a better balance.

Just as playtime is critical to your well-being, so is rest. Ideally we are most balanced when we work, play, and rest in equal measures. If you are lopsided in any of these, your psyche will suffer consequences. Since we're all different, it wouldn't be fair to say that these must be equally divided each day into eight-hour intervals. That wouldn't be very practical either for most people.

But averaged over a long period of time, all three should be fairly evenly divided. That also doesn't mean that all three are mutually exclusive activities. You may find your work to be like play. Sometimes play may feel like work, like if you're in a sports competition. Sometimes play is restful, like going to the movies or a classical music concert. Sometimes rest can be playful, like snuggling with someone you love on the couch and telling funny stories or tossing a ball to your dog.

Don't get caught up in labels. In general, work involves any activity with an agenda for productivity or an accomplishment of a necessary goal, like earning a living. Play provides pleasure and enjoyment without any real agenda except enjoyment. Rest rejuvenates the body, mind, and spirit to create more energy for work and play. All three support each other.

You need to determine the right balance for you. I was so inspired and excited about writing this book, that while many would view it as too much work along with a full-time practice, for me, it qualified as part of my play and rest time. This wasn't always the case, like when deadlines interfered with playtime with my daughter. But in the end, it's what I chose and I was glad to give up some needed rest for a temporary period to complete the challenge of writing. Sometimes, as when my daughter rightfully protested, I reminded myself of my grandest choice, to raise a child who felt loved and adequately cared for, and I put the writing aside to be with her. Believe me, I haven't always seen my behavior as choice-inspired, but I'm continuing to work on it, too.

Remember, you can change your priorities any time you wish. You might make one choice today only to discover tomorrow that it no longer works for you. Keeping your commitments is a very important component of emotional well-being, but not if doing so compromises your ultimate happiness and sanity.

Take a look at your day-to-day life and overall experience. Are you more heavily weighted in any one of the three areas of life: work, play, or rest? Are you fine with the imbalance? If not, challenge yourself to give something up so you can fulfill the area that's lacking.

Examine what you put into each of the three categories. For instance, some people consider cleaning their home to be an aspect of "play." They actually have fun doing it. For others, cleaning is a dreaded chore that they'd rather put off until the dust and clutter start hollering for their attention. Are the things you consider restful actually providing rest? Your body should be your best judge of that one.

When you claim your choices about how you work, rest, and play, life will seem much less about "shoulds" and "have-tos" and much more about desire and decision. Now, on to adopting healthy-hearted beliefs.

Chapter Twelve

Step Eight: Adopt New, Healthy-Hearted Beliefs

We've moved from the present to the past and back to the present. You've cleaned your closets, so to speak, and eliminated a wardrobe that no longer fits. You've kept the things that make you a unique individual and created room for new learning and growth opportunities. This stage is a vigorous process of self-acclamation, a series of personal pronouncements, a way of asserting ultimate control over your destiny. Now, instead of being reactive, it's time to become proactive as you champion your own best interests and defeat those attitudes dragging you down.

At the core of a sensitive heart lie faulty belief systems that lead you toward disaster over and over again. These are the five core faulty beliefs:

1. I am only of value when I'm in a relationship.
2. Other people's needs are more important than my own.
3. Other people are responsible for what I feel.
4. I have no control over my feelings.
5. I have to be nice to everyone, despite how they treat me.

By replacing each belief, you will shift from a wounded stance to one of ultimate empowerment. These changes will foster your ability to choose the life and relationships you want. You'll evolve from being sensitive-hearted to healthy-hearted.

You'll gain the power to greatly reduce the probability of attracting further injury from anyone.

TRANSFORMING SENSITIVE-HEARTED BELIEFS TO HEALTHY-HEARTED BELIEFS

Transforming belief systems can be a laborious effort. Once again, try to approach the evaluation of your beliefs from a place of curiosity, not judgment. The more open you are to acknowledging what is true of you, then the easier time you'll have with this transformation process.

HEALTHY-HEARTED BELIEF #1: I AM VALUABLE AND WORTHY, REGARDLESS OF WHETHER I HAVE A RELATIONSHIP TO VALI-DATE ME.

Changing your thinking from "I'm only of value when I'm in a relationship" to "I believe in my worthiness, regardless of my relationship status" puts you back in the driver's seat and, thus, back in control. You do not need others to endorse your inner value and worthiness of love or validation. Of course, you might prefer to have acknowledgment from others, but you don't require it. You can give it to yourself. Or you can seek it from people who have an available supply. While children need approval, validation, and admiration from their significant care-givers, adults do not need these strokes from others.

True, if you didn't get these emotional supplies you needed in childhood, they haven't been internalized and it's harder to give them to yourself in adulthood. Children who weren't wounded or whose wounds healed adequately automatically develop the capacity to care for themselves. They've received the essential equipment, so to speak.

In adulthood, when others aren't available to fulfill these needs, the well-cared-for adult simply draws upon the internal supplies and gives to herself what she needs. Others, whose childhood lacked some essentials, have to go against the grain. Internal messages direct them toward self-destruction or dependence on others. Adults with sensitive hearts must learn to give themselves what they didn't get. Practice giving these supplies to yourself, and before you know it, you'll no longer be dependent on others for their stamps of approval. Practice, practice, practice, until it becomes familiar and natural.

When you believe your value is contingent on being in a relationship, your sensitive heart directs you toward "desperate picking." You become hooked on anyone who shows even remote interest in you, leaving your needs and preferences out of the process. You don't ask enough questions. You don't pay close enough attention to disturbing actions or contradictions, and you're likely to be seduced by words even when there's no substance behind them. For instance, if you hear the words "I love you," you might disregard any actions that conflict with this statement.

If you only feel worthy when you're in a relationship, you'll be less likely to leave, even if the relationship becomes intolerable or your partner becomes downright abusive. You'll be afraid to end it because that would mean more than losing the relationship—you'd be losing your feelings of self-worth, since they depend on your being in the relationship. As you can see, this attitude fosters a destructive pattern.

Consequently, if your partner threatens to leave you, you'll be likely to promise anything to keep the relationship intact— even if that requires a major personality or behavioral overhaul. You'll refrain from expressing dissatisfaction with your mate's behavior. If you happen to voice criticism or complaint, you'll be quick to take it back, say you were only joking, or apologize or devalue the importance of your opinions, even if you delivered them in the kindest and gentlest way.

If you happen to find a loving partner, you might be afraid to deal with problems that even healthy couples routinely confront—like power struggles over who does what around the house or how to manage finances. What's more, you might inadvertently create situations where you sabotage a good connection or pick on things that don't really matter because you are so unfamiliar with feeling content. This belief affects more than your experience in intimate, romantic relationships. It may also undermine your friendships or work relationships.

Peter based his self-worth solely on his work performance and being liked by his boss. He stayed far too long in an exploitative work relationship. Without his connection to his boss, he didn't have anyone. He desperately needed this work relationship to fill the void in his life (or believed he needed it), so he tolerated the bad treatment. His boss expected him to work all hours of the day and night, never respected his privacy or right to a life outside of work, asked him to do meaningless errands that wasted Peter's time, only to harass him later for not meeting his deadlines.

Because Peter believed he needed this relationship to feel worthy, he failed from the start to do an adequate interviewing process. While he was asked hundreds of questions, he didn't ask even one about the job or what would be expected of him. It goes without saying that he never checked in with himself to see whether he could manage the job.

Eliminating the necessity to be in a relationship frees you to make connections with people who treat you with the love and respect you deserve.

HEALTHY-HEARTED BELIEF #2: MY NEEDS ARE EQUALLY AS IMPORTANT AS THE NEEDS OF OTHERS AND ARE THE MOST IMPORTANT TO ME.

By proclaiming this stance, even in extreme circumstances (such as becoming the victim of a crime), your survival needs take precedence over everything else. If it were in your best interest to accommodate your perpetrator, say, in order to preserve your life, then you would do that. If it were best to fight, you would do that. When someone truly renders you helpless, you still have the power to choose how to react to the state of helplessness.

When you start taking the absolute best possible care of yourself and believing in the importance of your needs, you create fewer situations where you will be a true victim again. And when you no longer hold yourself hostage to other people's needs, you can free others from being hostage to yours.

Keep in mind that there are very few situations in adulthood where you are ever completely a victim. As you've learned, children, especially younger ones, don't have the power to choose. They depend on adult caregivers to make adequate choices for them.

As adults, though, we no longer need to depend on others. We can provide for ourselves, even if we don't have conscious awareness or belief in our capacity for self-care. While adults sometimes place themselves in situations with only limited choices, there is almost always at least some power to choose.

The exceptions are when someone or something has full power over you, like a mugger pointing a gun or an earthquake. Under anything less than life-or-death circumstances, you have options.

Even in those cases, you still have the power to cut your losses. With the mugger, you could examine whether your choices increased your chances of being attacked, like the choices Annette made when she walked alone through a dark parking garage. In the case of the earthquake, you could ask whether you set yourself up with the greatest of earthquake preparedness. (I live in California, so I naturally think of earthquakes as natural disasters. You can fill in with whatever is more fitting to your location, like hurricanes or tornadoes.)

When you recognize your value and importance, you make fewer choices that threaten your safety or well-being and more choices in service of self-preservation and thriving.

If you hold the belief that other people's needs are more important, say to yourself, "Definitely not!" You may have learned early on that it can be emotionally or physically dangerous for you to take inventory of your own needs, preferences, and desires without first assessing someone else's. You may have been abandoned, shamed, or called "selfish" if you thought of yourself first. You may have learned that "selfish" is bad and "selfless" is good: a child's mind deals in black and white, with very little room for gray. You may have internalized this belief through your culture or religion or from your caregivers.

While critically important to children, acceptance from others cannot be as crucial for adults. If it is, you run a high risk of putting yourself in danger simply to avoid upsetting someone or losing acceptance.

You may also create an emotional hazard, wherein you constantly attend to other people and lose sight of yourself. This leaves you open to being resentful or in a chronic state of deprivation, both of which stress the body. We all know the costs of chronic stress: depression, anxiety, fatigue, and various physical maladies. People in a constant state of deprivation also run a greater risk of losing control of their own behavior and lashing out at others.

Nothing horrible will happen if you stop trying to please everyone. I'm not advocating that you stop taking other people's needs into account or stop caring about others. Nor should you completely disregard other people's opinions of you. Other people can provide very useful and valuable information that deserves your attention. This applies as long as you continue to stay connected to your own self and don't give all of your power away.

It's important to pay attention to your needs and to the needs of others. In fact, the converse belief—my needs are more important than those of others—can be equally ineffective in terms of developing true well-being.

Everyone's needs are important, but your needs are your primary responsibility. Once you can acknowledge the importance of your own needs, you can choose to decide where to place them in relation to others. Ideally, in your significant relationships, you'll create a balance.

When your needs and those of another clash, sometimes you'll opt for meeting your own. Sometimes you'll delay your own gratification to foster satisfaction in another person. If you live with or are involved with someone whom you fear will become aggressive if you stop servicing his or her needs, you must use all available resources to get out of the relationship safely. Consult a professional, go to a shelter, call the police, or employ whatever means are necessary to preserve your safety.

In this scenario, if you must placate this person temporarily in service of protecting yourself, then you are not revictimizing yourself. To the contrary, you would be acting with self-caring. The operative word is temporarily. This means you are acting in service of your safe escape, not out of a belief that the needs of others are more important than your own.

HEALTHY-HEARTED BELIEF #3: I AM RESPONSIBLE FOR MY OWN FEELINGS, AND OTHER PEOPLE ARE RESPONSIBLE FOR THEIR OWN FEELINGS.

Once you claim responsibility for your own feelings and disown responsibility for those of others, you'll recognize that influence does not equal cause. Your load will lighten considerably. You'll expect more of yourself, but you'll rid yourself of the burden of trying to be in control over something you have no power over. You won't be nearly as disappointed in others when they do not meet your expectations because you'll recognize that others don't cause your disappointment. One of the greatest indirect benefits of living this new belief is the elimination of unnecessary guilt.

Unnecessary guilt is the experience of wrongdoing based on a faulty assumption. If you believe you're responsible for someone's feelings and something you do means that person has "hurt" feelings, you're likely to experience guilt. But if you no longer hold this belief, when someone feels hurt, you'll recognize it's not your fault. You won't perceive that you've done something wrong. At the same time, you can still care about the impact of your actions or show concern.

I'm not advocating an uncaring approach to other people and their feelings. You still need to be accountable for your behavior. For instance, if you promise to tell the truth, but you tell a lie, you're accountable for that behavior. You have a role in creating a consequence for the person you lied to.

You don't need to go out of your way to knowingly hurt or offend those whom you love and care about, but you do need to stop being hostage to other people's reactions when they, too, have choices about how to feel. Feelings are a natural part of our human existence. Why should we be sheltered from our emotions or protect others from theirs? That would imply that feelings endanger us.

To this day, I've never known anyone to be injured by their feelings. Injury comes from the sometimes destructive ways in which people cope with their feelings. Even people who don't have sensitive hearts often hold the belief they are responsible for other people's feelings, but this belief almost always coexists with a sensitive heart.

If we are compassionate and caring individuals, the way other people feel, act, and think about us, especially those whom we value most, will certainly affect us. But precisely how we are affected is our choice. The effect is not caused by another person's behavior. People with sensitive hearts often have great difficulty distinguishing between feelings that are influenced by another person versus feelings that are caused by another.

Julie's mother blamed Julie for all of her negative feelings. Her mother said things like, "Julie, you make me so angry because you never listen," or "Because you didn't do your homework," or "Because you forgot to take out the trash."

Because, because, because, because. The list went on and on. Julie's mother really believed that Julie caused her to be angry. She didn't recognize that she was responsible for her own anger based on her perception of Julie's behavior and how she let it affect her.

Julie's mom couldn't see that Julie's behavior doesn't universally cause people to be angry. In fact, the same behaviors didn't even consistently evoke the same reaction in her mother. What angers one person may sadden another. While Julie's mother didn't have malicious intent, she was harming her daughter nonetheless. By not recognizing her own responsibility for her feelings, she passed this destructive belief along to her daughter.

Julie grew to share the belief that she caused other people's feelings. Naturally, she learned that if she caused other people's feelings, then other people must cause hers. She entered into a vicious cycle. She became a puppet, with other people's reactions determining her movements.

Young children don't have the capacity to regulate their own feelings. They're more reactionary. They haven't yet learned the necessary ingredients to healthy-hearted living. They haven't learned they can take charge of how they feel. They don't have to be puppets, but they must be taught to free themselves from this belief. So make sure that every day you practice taking responsibility when it does belong to you and letting go when it isn't yours.

HEALTHY-HEARTED BELIEF #4: I AM IN CHARGE OF HOW I FEEL AND HOW I CHOOSE TO ACT. OTHERS DO NOT MAKE ME FEEL OR BEHAVE IN ANY CERTAIN WAY. I MAKE THOSE CHOICES MYSELF.

Because feelings seem so automatic, it may seem strange at first to believe that you actually create your feelings. Most parents don't teach this to their kids, and society hardly teaches this lesson either. But how we feel about an event directly relates to our perceptions and the meaning we attach to it. We can change perception; therefore, we can change how we feel. It's that simple!

Let's say that as you read this, you perceive that I'm being too harsh, and you believe that harshness is unwarranted. Chances are you would feel angry or scared, in any case probably not happy.

But what if you get to know me better and you learn that I'm coming from a very caring and well-meaning place? Then you might perceive what I'm saying as valuable and beneficial to your growth. You probably won't be angry or scared anymore. You might even be intrigued and curious and feel pretty good.

Let's take another example. People often feel angry, sad, or scared when they believe they've been rejected. But rejection on its own doesn't necessarily have to equate with an unhappy feeling. What if you've invited someone to a party out of a sense of obligation, even though you really don't care much for that person? She calls to say she can't come. Yes, she has rejected your invitation. Will you feel happy or sad? My guess is that you would be happy.

The point is that our feelings about things are rarely universal. They are individual and customized to our own personal experience. They are the by-products of our thoughts, beliefs, and expectations.

People with sensitive hearts, however, often perceive that their feelings control their actions. But feelings don't prescribe action. They simply are part of our existence. They give us the sensation of life. We may choose a particular action based on a feeling, but we have options to choose other actions as well.

Just because I might be angry, doesn't mean I have to hit, scream, yell, or sulk. I could also elect not to be angry by examining my perception of whatever it is I got upset about.

My expectations could well be unrealistic, or I might be trying to control something I really don't have any control over. These are among the many possibilities of alternative actions.

Again, once you own your power to choose feelings and actions, you'll be far less likely to end up in situations where you victimize yourself. From a sensitive-hearted position, you might say, "I can't be happy because you keep hurting me."

However, once you adopt the healthy-hearted approach, you would take the following position: "I don't like the way you are treating me. I must leave this situation or ask you to change your behavior if you want me to stick around. My happiness is my choice, not your responsibility." Now you are free to leave a situation if you're not happy and take the action necessary to create your own contentment.

If this belief is new to you, try to keep feelings simple while you're still a novice at integrating and practicing it. While we have many words to describe feelings, keep the fancy ones to a minimum. Stay in tune with the four basics: mad, glad, sad, and afraid.

Often we confuse feelings with thoughts. Again, using rejection as an example, you cannot feel rejected. Rejection is an action. While you can perceive that you have been rejected, that doesn't describe how you feel about it.

Also, remember to keep shame and other unhealthy beliefs about your worthiness in another category. They are states of mind or beliefs that actually serve to keep us out of touch with our true emotions. For now, just notice your emotions and try to distinguish them from your thoughts.

If you start a sentence with "I feel that...," you aren't describing a feeling. Rather, you're describing a perception or thought. Nothing wrong with that, just don't deceive yourself into believing that you just shared a feeling.

HEALTHY-HEARTED BELIEF #5: I DO NOT HAVE TO BE NICE TO PEOPLE WHO TREAT ME BADLY. I CAN ASSERT MY RIGHT TO SAY "NO" TO MISTREATMENT.

Once you grant yourself permission to relax when confronted with the internal pressure to be nice, you'll have increased energy and compassion available for yourself and for the people who really care about your well-being and whose actions show it. You will deliver your good nature to those who have earned it.

Why should you be nice to everyone? What if someone treats you abominably? What if someone purposefully sets out to hurt you or repeatedly disregards your needs and feelings? It wouldn't make any sense to respond to these people the same as you would toward people who treat you kindly, gently, and respectfully. Sensitive-hearted people often don't understand their right to vary their responses according to the situation.

I'm hardly advising that you respond meanly or unkindly to ill-mannered people. But I strongly recommend that you build up a range of responses and choose those that apply to your interactions with others. It may make perfect sense to start out "nice," but if someone has treated you insensitively in the past, it would not be "adaptive" to stay nice. You should adapt your behavior to the situation. In this case, that means keeping your vulnerabilities to yourself and engaging with this person no more than necessary, if at all.

Two years divorced from a long marriage to a verbally unkind man, Helen continued to go out of her way to do nice things for him. When she baked cookies, she baked an extra batch for him, even though he never thanked her. When he was late on his support payments, she offered to help him out financially. He made twice the money she did but chose to gamble most of it away.

Helen remained as involved with him after the divorce as she was while they were married. He continued to exploit her nice gestures, and she continued to feel mistreated and betrayed.

She had to recognize that he wasn't going to change his actions any time soon. If she wanted to feel better, she had to change her behavior. Once she saw this option, she reined in on the kind gestures and adopted a firmer "I mean business" approach. He didn't like the change, but she understood that changing his behavior was not her job or her problem.

Unless your survival or safety is at stake, you can handle most unpleasant, rude, or even abusive interactions tactfully, without the need for reciprocal aggression. But under potentially violent circumstances, whatever gets you through the danger is warranted. Most often, though, if you confidently assert a firm boundary, you'll learn to quickly cut off any continued harassment.

Using the beliefs I've provided as a guideline, make a list of those you hold and those you need to change in your life to adopt the healthy-hearted version of each belief. Do you hold any I haven't included that may be keeping your wounds open and hurting?

Try changing the belief to a more healthy-hearted stance. The next time you feel mistreated, ask yourself which sensitive-heart belief might have been operative. When you put these healthy beliefs into effect, you should notice a sharp decline in how often or intensely you perceive you're being mistreated.

Chapter Thirteen

Step Nine: Love Your Body the Healthy-Hearted Way

Sometimes we forget about our physical being while working to heal our emotional wounds. People who carry old wounds are notorious for mistreating their bodies. They're predisposed to destructive and addictive behaviors, such as alcohol or drug abuse, eating disorders, sleep disorders, overwork, underwork, and so on. To become truly healthy-hearted, the sensitive-hearted must create a new relationship not only with other people but with their own bodies as well.

As someone with a sensitive heart, which is hopefully becoming more healed, you need to establish healthy rituals and routines that continuously reaffirm your inherent right and desire to thrive. Your body is the vehicle for the whole of your being, so you need to cherish and find the beauty in your physical form.

Without your awareness, unhealed wounds will direct you to treat your body in ways similar to how you were deprived as a child. You'll not be able to sustain any gains if you don't also address this residual re-creation of earlier wounds through your relationship with your body.

For instance, if you grew to consider your needs burdensome to others, then you will experience them as a nuisance whenever you notice them. Just as we develop psychological coping mechanisms to escape the experience of unwanted feelings or the shame attached to them, we develop ways to minimize the impact of our bodies' needs for attention.

Our bodies need a lot. They require ongoing checkups to make sure everything is in running order. Just like a car needs maintenance, if you don't service your body regularly, it's bound to eventually go kaput.

What may not be so easy for you is learning to read the cues your body constantly sends to tell you what it needs. After all, if you weren't adequately attended to as a child, you're likely to be more in the dark about how to provide the care you need. But unlike a car, which usually comes with a detailed owners' manual, your body doesn't come with a neatly packaged outline of what it needs. Besides, since your body is unique, no single manual would be sufficient.

You might have been given a general guideline of how to care for yourself, but you're going to have to modify it according to your special requirements.

WHAT YOUR BODY NEEDS FROM YOU

To function at its optimum level, your body needs food, water, exercise, rest, sleep, and soothing, pleasurable stimulation to all the senses, including touch, smell, taste, sight, and sound. While each of us will have our own requirements within these categories, everybody needs something from each. You must pay attention to all these elements and discover your own personal balance.

Most of all, your body needs your commitment to cherish it and pay close attention to its signals. This can be quite a challenge, especially if you were offered substitutes for your actual needs. For instance, if you were given candy to ease an emotional hurt because your caregivers weren't comfortable with emotional needs, then you're likely to confuse your needs for comfort with hunger. As an adult you might feed yourself when your body actually requires soothing.

Maybe no one valued your need for rest, and you were overly stimulated and kept busy with no time for leisure or play.

As an adult, you may overwork yourself or constantly take on projects to the point of exhaustion in denial of your body's signals to slow down.

It doesn't matter so much whether you can link the ways you deny your body's needs to childhood events. Rather, you need to observe the ways you mistreat your body today and make a commitment to enter a process of learning loving self-care.

COMMON WAYS PEOPLE WITH SENSITIVE HEARTS MISTREAT THEIR BODIES

1. Using self-prescribed, mood-altering substances to avoid or numb your actual experience. These may include drugs, alcohol, nicotine, or caffeine. I'm not saying that all use of these substances qualifies as mistreating the body. I'm sure the French would be appalled at the thought that regular enjoyment of wine is at all destructive. And, if you enjoy your cup or two of java, there's no need to worry. Neither is this a moral judgment. This isn't about wrong or right in the objective sense—it's more about understanding how you approach your body and whether you truly behave with care towards yourself. Do you neglect your needs? If so, ask yourself how much. What are the consequences to your body?

2. Using prescribed substances for something other than what they were prescribed for. This would include using pain medication to get high or increasing a dose of antidepressant medication to achieve euphoria rather than mood stabilization.

3. Eating too much for your body's optimal health. This has nothing to do with an aesthetic ideal for body weight. We're not talking size here; we're talking nutritional well-being. If you're eating more food than your

body requires, then you're probably feeding something other than hunger.

It would be more self-caring to attend to the needs you've mislabeled. Do you eat when you're tired, sad, anxious, or bored? No matter how much you eat, once you satiate your physical hunger, food cannot adequately nurture you through these other states. You might feel some temporary relief, but ultimately whatever you're ignoring will continue to press for your attention.

4. Eating too little to denounce your need for food to try to create the illusion of being in control or to appease a fear of getting fat. This may appear in extreme forms such as anorexia nervosa or, more subtly, as with perpetual dieting.

5. Eating for comfort instead of nutrition and not getting the necessary vitamins and minerals or a balance of carbohydrates, protein, and fat. Eating candy instead of a meal may taste great. But appealing solely to your sense of taste doesn't qualify as good self-care, especially at the expense of your body's nutritional needs.

6. Overexercising to escape some emotional state, like anxiety. There's nothing wrong with exercise. Like food, exercise is essential to optimum health. But you can have too much of a good thing, especially if it's motivated by self-judgment or self-attack or if you are substituting exercise for what you really need. It's great to want to run a marathon because it feels good. But if you're doing it because you hate your body and see the training as a way of burning so many calories that you'll lose weight so you won't hate yourself, then you're mistreating yourself.

As another example, if you go to the gym every time you feel some emotional discomfort rather than focusing on what really needs attention, you're using exercise as an avoidant strategy that will most likely someday backfire.

7. Underexercising. If you pile so much on your plate that you have no time or energy to put your body in motion, you ultimately deny yourself an essential component of your well-being. Exercise benefits the mind and the body. It energizes you and makes you better equipped to handle stress.

8. Ignoring your needs for medical attention when sick or injured. That's not to say you should run to the doctor with every sniffle or stomachache. But I can't tell you how many times I've seen people with potentially serious medical conditions fail to seek treatment. Sticking your head in the sand if something is possibly wrong with your health is seriously neglectful. If you have fears of doctors or medical procedures, you have to heal these. You must come to understand that the long-term consequences of not getting necessary treatment are far more serious.

9. Failing to get help for your emotional well-being if you're having trouble healing on your own. If you were raised to believe that you shouldn't share your problems with people outside your family or if you have bought into any of society's stigma about needing or desiring professional psychological treatment, you're likely to not seek help when you might really benefit from it.

   I understand that not everyone sees the benefit to psychotherapy or other methods of psychological healing. But again, if thriving is the goal, then therapy certainly needs to be one of the options, especially if other attempts aren't working.

10. Any behavior used to avoid dealing with underlying emotional issues, like overspending, excessive shopping, gambling, overwork, sex, video games, using the

Internet to avoid real social interaction, hyperactivity and inadequate sleep and/or too much sleep and rest.

These are not the only ways people mistreat their bodies. But they should give you some idea of what to look for in your own relationship with your body. Take a moment now. Using the above descriptions as a guideline, identify those you're most familiar with. If you have other ways not listed above, note those, too.

FIVE STEPS TO BODY WELLNESS

STEP ONE:

Commit to making the care of your body your number-one priority. Just as you made a commitment not to put yourself in situations where revictimization is likely, it's time to make a pledge to treat your body with love and respect.

STEP TWO:

Imagine your body as an infant who is completely dependent on you for survival and the ultimate experience of contentment. You wouldn't let an infant go hungry because you have other things you want or even have to do. Your infant's hunger would take priority over your "to do" list. First things first. If you have ever cared for an infant, you'll know that you go through a checklist when trying to decipher what a cry means. The list would look something like this: hungry, wet, tired, overstimulated, understimulated, sick, frustrated, and so on. The order doesn't matter as much as the attempt to cover all the bases. As an adult, your checklist has expanded. But in the expansion, you might have ignored the basics. If you look at your body as like an infant, it will help remind you to attend to the basics first.

STEP THREE:

Pamper yourself every day for at least fifteen minutes in a way that meets the needs you tend to ignore. For instance, if you have a high-energy workday, your body needs something restful and soothing by the end of the day. Take a bath, read a book, listen to soft music, light candles, rub your body with lotion, get a massage, or soak your feet. If your children demand your attention all day, find a few minutes of solitude to reclaim your body as your own. Little ones, especially, will treat your body as if they own it. While it's your job not to shame them for this, you must also make some time to separate yourself, even if it's only for a few minutes.

If you tend to spend your days mostly in isolation, then create time for social interaction and the comfort of other people's company. If you don't find comfort in being with other people, you probably have to look at the relationships you've created and whether you need to create better ones with new people (more on this in the next chapter). You may have trust issues that you need to face so that you can get something from other people.

Remember the key to a healthy relationship with your body is to respect all its needs. If your life is filled with intellectual energy, you might need more balance on the emotional, spiritual, and sensual levels. If you're invested in a more emotional or caregiving world, your body may need more intellectual stimulation. Balance is the key.

STEP FOUR:

Practice breathing and relaxation techniques on a regular basis. Try yoga, meditation, or stretching. For years you've been carrying wounds and sensitivities that have continued to hurt you consciously or unconsciously. These were not housed in an isolated part of your brain. The energy of the wounds has been recirculating through your entire system, leaving toxic residue. It's common for sensitive hearts to have a physical manifestation of emotional pain in forms like migraine headaches, backaches, muscle tension, high blood pressure, ulcers, chronic fatigue, agitation, irritable bowel syndrome, and so on. Breathing and relaxation techniques help reduce the stress on the body from the emotional distress you've been housing.

If you've lived with chronic discomfort and physical distress, these methods may not seem effective right away. Don't give up prematurely or decide they have no value. Incorporate one or all of these activities into your daily ritual of self-care. Your body will eventually thank you. If you have any suspicion of a physical illness, you should certainly consult with a physician before embarking on any technique that may harm you.

STEP FIVE:

Practice adoration of your physical form. Hating or picking on one's physical form is such a frequent by-product of a sensitive heart. People become obsessed with what they consider their body flaws as an unconscious means of avoiding the belief that one's inner self is flawed and damaged.

Women especially, but men also in increasing numbers, attack body parts for not being what they consider to be perfectly formed. They've forgotten that the body is a vehicle for expressing our inner selves. They buy in to the illusion that they'll be more lovable if they can change the appearance of their thighs or hips. Some people go to the extreme of cosmetic surgery, but regardless, they discover that none of these methods actually heals the inner hurt.

I'm not saying anything is wrong with improving yourself physically if that will make you happy. Just make sure you are operating from a place of choice and awareness and that you are choosing the best solution to the problem. If you have low self-worth because deep inside you believe you are unworthy of love, no amount of plastic surgery will help.

THE MIRROR EXERCISE

Using the following mirror exercise will help you make peace with your whole body. It is aimed to help you stop obsessing on your outside physical form and free the energy you need to heal from the core. Start with the part of your body that you pick on the most, whether that's your stomach, thighs, arms, nose, or ears. Stand in front of the mirror naked. Take a good long look at this part of your body. As you're looking, repeat to yourself these words:

> *Thank you my _____ (fill in with the part of your body you've chosen) for being an important part of my body. I would not be able to _____ (fill in with the function that body part provides) without you. I will start loving and respecting you from here on as you are a gift I am so fortunate to have.*

For instance, if you pick on your stomach, wishing it were flatter, you would thank your stomach instead for the beauty of digestion.

Next, touch that part of your body and feel the texture of it. Use only positive words to describe it. This will be hard at first, especially if you've been prone to attacking it. Welcome this body part back into your life. Stop alienating it as if it were an animal with rabies. It's there to serve you, so be nice to it. Go through the above method for each body part you tend to alienate. This will help you stop treating your body like an enemy.

You'll never truly be free to allow someone to fully love you if you can't love your own body. Even if someone tries and truly sees your beauty inside and out, if you attack your body, you will ultimately destroy any positive feedback from someone else. Treat your body the way it deserves, with care and respect. Cherish it and make it your best friend. You won't be getting another one, so make peace with the one you have.

Chapter Fourteen

Step Ten: Set Boundaries to Create Healthy-Hearted Relationships

Every healthy heart stays healthy by setting good boundaries. People with sensitive or bruised hearts, however, often suffer great difficulty and confusion about how to set and manage boundaries.

Trisha's mom stayed at home until Trisha began preschool at age four. Before she returned to work, she and Trisha did everything together. But when she returned to her job, responsibilities often consumed her time and energy, and Trisha experienced a deep sense of abandonment. Because the change happened so abruptly, Trisha didn't have time to make the transition smoothly. She was at the peak of her struggle, wanting constant connection with her mom yet simultaneously yearning to explore her world as her own separate person.

It's important to remember that for so many children, wounds come from well-meaning parents. Trisha's mother believed returning to work would be the best for everyone. She wasn't attuned to how much Trisha needed her. And even if she was more aware, she may have chosen to return to work anyway because other needs of the family's were also important.

Nevertheless, Trisha's developmental needs were unintentionally compromised. At first she was the sole fulfillment for her mother, with her dependency reinforced, then later it was reinforced only for independent strivings. It wasn't necessarily her mother's return to work that caused the issues, but rather that she didn't know to soothe her daughter's distress. Had the mother been more keyed into the developmental process, she could have dealt more sensitively with the impact on her daughter and possibly prevented some of the wounds that resulted.

Because of her underlying fear of abandonment, in her adult relationships, Trisha felt compelled to cling to contact, even when she truly craved moments of separate space.

THE DEVELOPMENT OF
OPTIMAL BOUNDARIES

Boundaries form through maturation and development. Through these processes, we come to recognize ourselves as separate (via physical boundaries), unique individuals (via psychological boundaries). The process is innate. Under optimal conditions, it proceeds in a sequence that leads to a healthy self-concept, allowing us to feel connected and belonging without losing our experience of separateness and uniqueness.

We start out in the world without physical or psychological boundaries. We don't really have a sense of where we start or stop in relation to our caregivers. We are completely, "symbiotically" attached to them. As motor skills develop, however, we become more and more tolerant and desirous of separateness.

By the time an infant can walk, he can usually regulate the distance he wants from others. If left to his preference, this distance is not very great at first. But as the infant's sense of self develops and he gains more confidence, his capacity to tolerate physical distance increases, as seen when he becomes a toddler.

For healthy development to ensue, in the first year of life an infant needs to be allowed complete attachment and dependency on a caregiver for everything but what nature provides reflexively, like breathing. If the primary caregiver can't tolerate this, the process becomes arrested. The precise impact is impossible to predict. Most likely, there will be problems later in the area of attachment and the capacity to experience oneself as a separate, unique individual. It may also be that the awareness of separateness creates anxiety.

As time passes, in an ideal world (which we all know doesn't exist), the infant begins to recognize that she is a separate being from the caregiver. While the need to separate and individuate is innate, the process comes with tremendous ambivalence. The caregiver's response needs to be particularly gentle and empathetic.

Frustrating an infant's need for gratification is a necessary by-product of the awareness of a differentiated self. It need not be traumatic if the caregiver remains sensitive to the process. With the awareness of physical separateness, the infant begins to experience independence from the caregiver, with recognition like "My body is mine" and "I have my own feelings and thoughts."

If a caregiver carries unresolved boundary issues or doesn't understand the process of differentiating, these may be projected onto the infant and complicate the process.

At one extreme, a caregiver may be terrified of the infant's complete dependency and prematurely force the child into independence. On the other extreme, a caregiver may fear the infant's normal, healthy need to be separate. Consequently, this caregiver may smother and engulf the child in an attempt to maintain the dependency.

Many caregivers experience both fears simultaneously, or they may shift back and forth between them, depending on the state of their own personal self-fulfillment.

Optimal boundaries require you to accept the whole range of your inner needs, from dependence to independence. They remain flexible enough to change according to the specifics of a situation. They remain permeable enough to permit intimacy, yet not so permeable that they engender a loss of self. They have the capacity to become rigid and inflexible if necessary to keep you from harm.

Optimal boundaries work for you rather than against you. They're set according to both your inner needs and the demands of a situation.

If you have a fear of your own independent strivings, whether conscious or unconscious, your boundaries may tend to be very loose and fluid. This will serve you well in situations requiring closeness and intimacy. However, if you have a difficult time strengthening them when a situation calls for more distance and caution, you may be at a disadvantage. On the other hand, if you have a fear of your needs for closeness and dependency, your boundaries may be more difficult to penetrate. If so, you may do well in situations that require you to be guarded and more cautious.

But trouble relaxing your boundaries may mean you miss out on the comfort of close intimate contact. When you resolve and make room for the whole range of your needs, you enable yourself to shift along the continuum of permeability. This applies to both your physical and psychological boundaries.

Those with highly permeable boundaries tend to be open and receptive. They often describe themselves as very trusting and desirous of intimacy. However, if this tendency is not coupled with a capacity for firmer boundaries, these people are often easily hurt and surprised when others take advantage of them. They often open up to people who have not yet earned their trust. Sometimes they do this out of fear that they will otherwise be shut out and alone. They may believe that the only alternative is to be rigid and closed. That belief magnifies their fear that there are only two alternatives, either to live in the world with high openness and endure a high risk of hurt or to prevent the risk of hurt by living in the world sheltered and alone. The second option is really no alternative at all, because being alone is intolerable for those who fear separateness.

The need for intimacy is real. It would be there regardless of the fear of separateness. But some of the need for it serves as a shield from fear. If this description fits for you, then you need to make room for a third alternative in which you permit yourself to acknowledge the whole range of your needs and then set your boundaries accordingly.

Those with more rigid and inflexible boundaries tend to be more suspicious of others, more guarded and self-protective. They often fear they will lose their individuality and become engulfed by another person's needs if they get too close. They often describe themselves as needing a lot of space, especially when involved in an intimate relationship that requires more contact. They fear their own dependency needs.

Those who are more stuck on this end of the continuum also tend to experience only two alternatives. If they become intimate and flex their boundaries, they fear a loss of self. If they stay guarded and completely unattached, the fear of engulfment is contained, but the potential of deep, beneficial, intimate contact sharply decreases, if it is not forsaken altogether.

If this more aptly describes you, your task is to identify and work through your fears of intimacy so that you can become more in charge of where and how you set your boundaries.

How do you know on which end of the continuum you tend to set your boundaries? Generally speaking, no one sits exclusively on one end or the other. In some areas in your life, you have probably mastered pretty effective boundaries while in other areas you're either too rigid or too permissive. But you may still find that you dominantly rest on one end or the other. In that case, that would be the place to start your focus.

Here are some examples of boundaries meant to help you assess where to focus your attention. Let's say that a friend calls to talk about a problem she's having. You have an important day tomorrow that requires you to get plenty of rest. You care deeply for your friend, but past experience tells you you'll be talking to her for at least an hour. A conversation that long would not be in your best interest and might jeopardize your upcoming important day.

What do you tell your friend?

A. "I wish you would stop bothering me with your problems. Can't you tell I'm busy?"

B. "I'm sorry, but tonight really isn't a good time for me. Maybe we can talk tomorrow."

C. "I can talk for a little while, but I have to go in thirty minutes."

D. Same as (C), but instead of hanging up when you said you would, you keep listening until your friend feels she's finished.

E. "I can listen as long as you want me to. I'm sure it's more important than anything I have to do."

This is an exercise without a right answer, but I think you will find that choices (A) and (E) are on the extremes. With choice (A), virtually no attention is paid to the feelings of your friend. This response reflects an entirely "me" point of view. You may feel you've had enough of your friend's woes, but unless you've already had a discussion making her privy to what's going on in your head, you are holding her accountable for the difficulty you have setting boundaries for yourself.

Choice (A) would be a fitting response to a request from someone who has blatantly disregarded your repeated attempts to make your needs known.

Choice (E) pays no attention at all to your own needs. It renders you a slave to your friend's needs. With this choice, you set up a situation where you expect your friend to read your mind to divine your actual needs. If you're prone to setting your boundaries in terms of other people's needs, you need to focus more attention on yourself. You must learn to regulate your needs with yourself in mind, as well.

Choice (D) attempts a balance between self and others. But since you don't follow through on the boundary you set, you lose your credibility, setting yourself up to not be taken seriously. If during the conversation you determine that your friend is in a true crisis, and you therefore decide you're willing to extend your boundary, that's no problem. That's a matter of conscious choice, which is different from continuing to listen because you don't believe you have the right to end the call.

Given this particular situation, I consider choices (B) and (C) as the most balanced and the choices that best serve healthy boundary-setting. That doesn't mean the other choices have no place in the world. On some occasions in your life, it may be best to have really loose boundaries, like in an intimate moment with a love partner (during lovemaking, perhaps, or when sharing your most vulnerable secrets). Other times, the most rigid boundaries will be your best choice, like when you've been hounded by a telemarketer regarding a product you have no use for and your seven polite attempts to end the call have failed. A response like "Don't call me again!" might be exactly what the doctor ordered. But, an immediate negative reaction to anyone trying to sell you something, even if the person is polite, may indicate that you are displacing pent-up resentment on anyone who gets in your way. The key to optimal boundaries involves consciousness, choice, acceptance of the whole range of needs, and the ability to flex according to each situation.

BOUNDARY-STRENGTHENING EXERCISES

Boundaries are like muscles. You want them to be strong enough to protect, defend, and support you. You also want them to relax when you are in a restful and safe place. There are two images I like to use to help strengthen your boundary-setting capacity: the ladder image and the bank teller image.

THE LADDER IMAGE

Picture yourself on a ladder. Each rung represents a new level of boundary, where the bottom rung is the most flexible and the top is the least. When you interact with people, imagine you are positioned in the middle of the ladder ready to proceed. The direction you take, upward or downward, will depend on what you discover when you check in with yourself about what you need and what is available to you in your surroundings. Once you determine the direction, you can experiment with different degrees of firmness along the way.

Let's say that at the end of the day you feel tired and in need of rest. But you're committed to having dinner with an old friend who's only in town for a weekend. You've been looking forward to the dinner, but your body is telling you to lie down and take a nap. The middle rung of the ladder would be equated with something of a neutral position. From this position, you can make a good case for going to the dinner. After all, you've been looking forward to it and you enjoy your friend's company. You could also make a good case for not going. You're exhausted and, because of that, you don't think you would be such good company and you would really rather rest.

Now it's time to ask yourself what is in your best interest if it made absolutely no difference to your friend. Next, ask your friend how he would feel if you were to cancel. If you would rather stay home and your friend doesn't mind, then there is no conflict and the decision is easy. But if your need is in conflict with your friend's, then the situation requires attention to your boundaries.

Regarding the boundaries you set for yourself, first ask how strict you need to be with yourself around rest. Remember from chapter seven, you need to balance your work, play, and rest. Is it typical for you to adhere to a sleep pattern that you virtually never alter? Would it really be a problem if you loosened up a little? If you rigidly restrict yourself, then I would suggest you consider going to dinner unless you really feel it would be detrimental to your health.

If, on the other hand, you rarely pay attention to your needs for rest, you might consider honoring your exhaustion even if it would disappoint your friend. Or you could make a deal with yourself to go this time but to pay better attention to getting enough rest the next time you're booking your social calendar. Weighing all of these possibilities and many I haven't included gives you greater access to all rungs on the ladder.

In general, the top of the ladder represents the firmest boundary, even to the level of aggression. This level is best reserved for people and situations that pose a threat to either your physical or psychological safety. Under threatening conditions, you may not even move slowly up the ladder but might jump straight to the top.

For instance, you would have a "no questions asked" policy if you were to see someone with a gun. You would leave the scene immediately. And if you were in a car and someone approached you pointing a gun, you might accelerate right into the person in order to protect yourself.

The bottom of the ladder represents the most malleable of boundaries. This level is best reserved for situations in which you feel completely safe and trusting. An example might be if you were feeding a baby or on a meditative retreat.

THE BANK TELLER IMAGE

Imagine yourself as the owner of a bank where you are the only bank teller. Picture yourself behind a Plexiglas window with a tray for passing things back and forth between you and your customers. Your customers include anyone with whom you have interactions. They could be strangers, family members, or other loved ones. Since you own the bank, you hold the only key to all areas.

Use this image to help you get more comfortable at setting boundaries. Imagine that with each interaction, people come to your window. Depending on the person, it may be best to do the entire transaction at the window where you do all exchanges through the window, using the tray. The Plexiglas offers a boundary firm enough to protect you if necessary yet flexible enough that you can see and hear your customers.

You are in charge. If someone deposits something in the tray you don't want, you can give it back or simply leave it there. If you want to share more of your bank, you can do so at any time. If you decide to keep the person more at a distance or away completely, you can limit the customer's banking privileges or close the account completely.

This image is particularly useful for people who believe they have a right to something of yours when in reality they don't, that is, people with excessive entitlement. For instance, if you were raised in a family with very loose boundaries, where separateness and individuation weren't particularly honored, you may find it hard to take care of your own needs in the face of the needs of others.

Alex's parents expected him to come over for dinner at least once a week to continually remind them that he loved them. Though Alex was thirty years old with a busy schedule and family of his own, his parents persisted in treating him like a little boy. If he made it over for dinner, in their eyes he was a "good boy"; if he didn't, he was a "bad boy." After many years of complying with his parents' wish, he grew to resent them. But he was too guilt-ridden to disappoint them and too afraid of their reaction if he set limits with them.

Alex found the bank teller image particularly helpful. With it, he lovingly told his parents he was no longer able to commit to dinner each week. He would make efforts to see them as his schedule permitted. As he predicted, they had great difficulty understanding or accepting his boundary. He placed their reaction on the tray, looked it over, and decided to hand it back to them. He indicated that he was sorry they were displeased, and he hoped that someday they would grow to appreciate that he had his own life now. He welcomed them to join him in his world. He realized he was no longer a little boy dependent on their approval. Quite frankly, if they didn't like the adult he'd become, they didn't have to be part of his life. He allowed himself his own choices and left them to make their own choices.

Initially, Alex was quite reluctant and a little bit afraid to stand up to his parents. He did love them, but he no longer bought into their definition of love. Eventually, his parents came around and understood his need for space. Though they certainly made a lot of noise at first, Alex patiently yet persistently held his ground.

When you practice setting boundaries, try to experiment at first with people and places where the consequences won't matter very much to you. For instance, maybe the next time you're in line and someone tries to step in front of you, try a different response from what you would normally do.

If you're prone to silencing yourself, try to speak up. Say something like, "Excuse me, maybe you didn't notice, but the line begins behind me." Don't push it if the person becomes hostile. It's generally not a good idea to match belligerence with belligerence, as this usually escalates a situation. If, on the other hand, you tend to become aggressive and quick-tempered whenever anyone steps on your toes, try to loosen up a bit. Tone down your typical response with a little more politeness and understanding.

Once you experiment with inconsequential people and situations, I encourage you to slowly progress to those that are more meaningful. You will eventually discover that many people respond quite well to your improved boundaries. You may even see that you command more respect from others and from yourself. In practicing optimal boundary setting, you may also discover that you have more energy available and less resentment toward others. You'll become more forthcoming with your needs and more self-responsible.

THE RELATIONSHIP COST-BENEFIT ANALYSIS

Optimal boundaries permit healthy-hearted relationships, but they don't ensure them. Sometimes you will make changes, and your current relationships won't be able to weather the changes. In order to maintain your growth, you will have to build a loving and supportive cast of people in your life.

Some people may need to be eliminated altogether or, at the very least, excluded from your inner circle. If you surround yourself with people who don't reinforce your gains or who might actively sabotage them, you could lose most, if not all, of your progress.

Evaluating your relationships in terms of what they provide for you may seem scary. It's one thing to have to make changes in yourself, but now I'm encouraging you to assess your entire support network. I hope you won't be too alarmed. For the most part, this will probably be a natural by-product of improving your own internal support. Once you feel good about yourself, it will be easier to make these changes if they are necessary to maintain your progress.

As you heal your sensitive heart, you'll also become far better at creating new relationships with people who have the capacity to aid and support your growth. You'll no longer be tempted to go to an empty well for water or a hardware store for your groceries. Instead, you'll find a full well and you'll go to the market when you need food and the hardware store when you need a hammer and nails.

For now, however, you need to assess your current relationships. Decide which are worth keeping as they are, which to keep if changes are made, and which you may need to separate from altogether.

If you have felt wounded by the people who cared for you and the wounds have remained unhealed, it's highly likely that you've re-created these wounds in your adult relationships. As you continue your healing process, some of these relationships simply won't serve your needs anymore. They'll either have to change or you'll probably want to end them, hopefully without too much mayhem.

Relationships have many components and come in many varieties. We all have many colors and shades to our personalities and our behavior, and we need to be cautious about making blanket judgments or generalizations about others. However, if there are people in your life who persistently mistreat you, can't support you, or blatantly abuse you, you must address this if you're going to thrive. The actual methods you will use to address someone whom you feel mistreats you will depend on several variables. How important is the person to you? What would the consequences really be (as opposed to what you fear they would be) if you were to sever the relationship?

Let's say a close friend gets really angry with you, calls you a hurtful name, and then doesn't talk to you for three days. You might feel hurt or annoyed and believe you've been wronged, and your feelings would be understandable. However, before acting on these feelings and determining that the friendship is permanently damaged, you might ask yourself whether this is unusual behavior from your friend. What happened between the two of you? Maybe you have a role in the reaction and maybe not. In any case, you would need to examine that possibility.

On the other hand, does your friend typically lash out at you and then withdraw? Are you the target of her anger even when you've truly not been provocative? If you answer "yes" to these questions, then you would want to really evaluate this friendship.

Are you familiar with this kind of behavior in others? What might you be re-enacting from your childhood? After assessing the relationship, you can decide whether the incident is worth addressing directly with her. You can set boundaries around what is and isn't acceptable behavior. Then, depending on the response, you can determine whether the friendship is worth continuing. In essence, you need to ask yourself if you really need this relationship and why. To help you assess your relationships, try the following exercise—the relationship cost-benefit analysis.

Step One. Make a list of all your significant relationships in the present. Make sure to include all types of relationships, including those with parents, siblings, other relatives, friends, lovers, and coworkers.

Step Two. For each person on your list, ask yourself and answer the following questions:

1. Do you have contact with this person mainly out of obligation or out of desire?
2. If you really desire the contact, ask, "Is this person truly a source of comfort and support to me, and do I feel cared about?"
3. If you answered "yes," move on to the next person and start at number one. If you answered "no," ask yourself this. Do you think the person would be willing and able to make changes that would lead to a more fulfilling relationship, and is the person worth your effort? By the way, you would probably need to make changes also.
4. List the benefits and the cost for keeping the relationship. Also list the benefits and costs of minimizing or ending the contact.

5. If you decide the relationship is worth keeping but that it needs some adjustment to be more fulfilling, use the tools you've learned about setting boundaries and asking for what you need. If you decide the relationship isn't worth the effort, then you need to work on ending the contact.

If you've made attempts to alter or sever a relationship but have not been successful, ask yourself "why." Would the change put you in any physical or psychological danger? If the answer is "yes," seek professional help immediately. Don't attempt anything that may resemble a confrontation with the potential to endanger you. If the answer is "no," ask yourself what you imagine the consequences would be. Are you afraid of something you're imagining? Are your fears likely to come true? As adults, we need things from other people, but we're not dependent on any one person the way we were as children. If a relationship doesn't supply you with what you desire and crave, make room for new ones that will.

Once you've identified your fears, challenge yourself a bit further. Instead of stopping at your first discovery, ask yourself again what you fear. Then ask yourself "And then what?" until you've reached your bottom-line catastrophe. Ending a relationship really doesn't entail any catastrophe. You may hurt for awhile, but it certainly won't kill you to let go of unfulfilling relationships.

Once you've answered all of the above questions, make a decision about how to proceed, and then implement your plan.

As you've learned, we all need social contact and intimacy in our lives. But as an adult, you are free to choose the people in your social sphere. Stay aware of your reactions to others and examine their source (i.e., from old unhealed wounds, from the current relationship or situation, or from a combination of the two). And always stay willing to look at your part in creating distress.

Chapter Fifteen

Step Eleven: Graduation Day

Congratulations! You've got all the essentials for healthy-hearted living. Now it's time to stand up and make a formal declaration of your right to thrive. Just like Dorothy in *The Wizard of Oz*, who always had the power to go home, you have always had the power to thrive.

Like Dorothy's magic slippers, your power has been with you all along. You just needed to find it—buried beneath a sensitive heart. As long as you travel along your healing path, you will continue to awaken and solidify this power, never again to return to the prison of a bruised or sensitive heart. You're free to embrace the whole of your life experience. Your sensitive heart has become a strong yet deeply compassionate, happy heart.

Do the following exercise to help you celebrate your victory over the past, solidify the changes you've created, and reinforce your motivation to maintain the changes. Don't cut any corners on this one! The more effort you put into it, the more benefit you'll reap.

DECLARATION OF YOUR RIGHT TO THRIVE

You'll need paper and pen. If you must, use a computer. You'll also need colored markers, pencils, or crayons to decorate your document. If you hold the belief that you are a lousy artist, toss it out the window. Your artistic talent or skill has no bearing on your ability to do this exercise effectively. In fact, the less you rely on preprinted or decorated paper, and the more you allow for your own creative expression, the more benefit you'll get.

There's a reason I'd rather you didn't use a computer. You might find this exercise more valuable if you draw upon your pool of creative energy, which connects you more closely to the experience of being younger. Through the act of writing, coloring, and decorating without the aid of a computer, you'll reconnect with the most vulnerable parts of yourself, the parts that have far too long housed your unhealed wounds.

STEP ONE

Feel free to modify or adapt this language so the declaration really applies to you. On a piece of the best quality paper you have, write the following:

DECLARATION OF MY RIGHT TO THRIVE

1. I was in no way responsible for the mistreatment I endured in childhood.
2. I did not deserve to be _____. (Name whatever ways you perceive that you were mistreated, such as hit, molested, insulted, shamed, yelled at, neglected, abandoned, oppressed, ridiculed, etc.)
3. Now I'm an adult, and I no longer have to tolerate being victimized by anyone, not even myself.
4. I must mourn the losses of my childhood and adulthood and all that I did not get.
5. I am lovable and worthy of having all of my basic needs met.
6. I'm a good person and worthy to be who I am and to live the life I was meant to live.

7. I'm entitled to self-expression and the fullest possible development of my gifts.
8. I can take charge of my behavior in the present and create the future I desire.
9. There is nothing preventing me from becoming a Thriver once I get out of my own way.
10. Each and every day I will claim my right to live, love, and be loved.

STEP TWO

Decorate the surrounding space on your paper with whatever appeals to you. Use flowers, crayons, markers, stickers, or whatever you like. Make it a work of art. Do not skimp on time or energy. What you put into this is a statement of your value.

STEP THREE

Hang your "Declaration of My Right to Thrive" where you will see it many times a day. (If you have children and do not want them to see this because they may not be developmentally ready to know about your stuff, then keep it private. If you keep it private, don't forget to read it to yourself.)

STEP FOUR

Read your declaration at least three times a day for two weeks and after that at least once a day until it feels like an integral part of you. Formally creating your declaration enhances its meaning. The official aspect makes it more real. It expresses commitment to your growth, and it honors who you are and all that you deserve. Don't shortchange yourself by just reading the exercises in this book. You'll reap much more benefit if you actually do them.

Thriving is an ongoing process. Regression into old patterns is to be expected. But once you've tasted life as a Thriver, you'll want nothing less. You will come to recognize slips into old behavior sooner and be able to shift gears back into new behavior more quickly. Practice what you've learned throughout this book, and implement your new tools wherever you can. Before you know it, thriving will become the only way of life you'll ever choose again.

A SPECIAL NOTE TO PARENTS

First of all, it's impossible to be able to escape wounding your kids at times. Nobody is perfect, and no one can fully predict the impact something will have on a child no matter how well you know him or her.

Sometimes a behavior will have a positive influence. Other times, depending on your child's mood, age, tiredness level, and so on, the very same behavior may seriously upset your child and create the makings of a sensitive heart.

Learning how to best care for your particular child is a constant evolutionary process. Just when you think you have figured it all out, a new developmental phase will kick in and throw you for a loop.

The good news is that children are extraordinarily resilient. While we have a responsibility as parents to be accountable for our actions toward our children, we need to leave ourselves some room for error. What's most important is admitting when you've hurt your child and taking responsibility for it.

More than anything in the world, your children want to love you. They want to hold you in a positive light. Make it easier for yourself and for them by claiming your mistakes. Even if you don't agree with your child's perception of how you behaved, you always have room to empathize with their feelings.

After you show compassion for what your child feels, you might want to have a discussion about your intentions or what you think actually happened. Pay attention to your children, and they will tell you what they need. If you're having problems with your parenting, seek help. It's rarely too late to repair a wound with your own child if you really come from a place of genuine compassion.

Don't resent your children if you can offer them what you didn't get. By giving them what they need, you will be giving both yourself and them the best gift of all—the inherent right to thrive and have healthy-hearted relationships.

So before you declare your right to thrive, make amends to your kids. If you don't have kids, make a vow to play a role, no matter how small, in preventing the potential wounding of future generations. Remember, children need all adults to be accountable.

Resources

Countless resources exist for additional help from books, support groups, online services, psychotherapy, and seminars. While selfhelp such as this book may be enough for many sensitive-hearted people, it probably won't suffice for those with serious wounds or those suffering other symptoms like depression, addiction, anxiety, nightmares, or phobias.

As you've learned, Thrivers use all available resources. If their internal resources don't lend enough support, they seek outside help. If you're not feeling better or if you desire even more support and assistance than you've received from reading this book, take a look at what else is out there for you. Below are a few suggestions on where and how to look for additional self-help resources.

I strongly recommend the book *Authoritative Guide to Self Help Resources in Mental Health*, by J.C. Norcross et al. (New York: Guilford Press, 2000). This comprehensive guide covers resources addressing many issues related to sensitive hearts like depression, child development and parenting, addictions, eating disorders, love and intimacy, and stress management. It even offers ratings for each source of help and provides recommendations for support groups, online services, books, and movies.

If you feel you would benefit from more personal professional help, again there are numerous options. If financial limitations keep you from seeking therapy, keep in mind that many therapists offer their services when warranted at a lower fee or know of someone who does. Many communities have clinics or training institutes that offer professional counseling at a reduced fee. If you don't know how to find what you need, I recommend the following avenues:

1. Contact your county or state psychological association for a list of qualified therapists in your area.
2. Ask your physician for a referral to a mental health professional in your area.

3. If you have health insurance, call to find out about out-patient mental health benefits. If you are covered, the company should provide you with a list of providers in your area.
4. Contact local hospitals for a list of referrals.
5. Ask for a referral from a friend or anyone whom you trust who has had a positive therapy experience. The person your friend saw would be a good one to call for a referral. (Keep in mind that many therapists will not accept clients who are friends or relatives of other clients whom they have treated. This serves to protect confidentiality and boundaries. But the therapist should be able to provide names of other practitioners.)

If you do choose to get into some kind of therapy, make sure to interview your potential therapist. It's very important to find someone who makes you feel safe. Finding a good fit will help you to reap the best benefit. That means someone who knows about the issues you struggle with. Be patient. Sometimes the search can take a little while.

Most importantly, I wish for you a healthy heart and all the goodies that come along with that. Healing, learning, and growth involve a life-long process. If you stay on the path of life, your present and future will continue to inspire you!

Appendix

RELATIONSHIP Q AND A

I thought your thriving journey might be enhanced if you had some examples of real-life questions and conflicts people with sensitive hearts routinely face in their adult relationships. The following questions, which appeared in my column Dear Dr. Debra, came from sensitive-hearted people who wished to end the cycle of re-creating old wounds and develop a path to healthy-hearted relationships. These letters and my responses highlight the themes and concepts I've presented throughout the book. As a sensitive-hearted soul, I often see a mirror reflection of myself in the problems of those who write to me. It is my deepest wish that you, too, will find value in what's reflected and gain a sense of peace, knowing that you are not alone in your journey!

Dear Dr. Debra,

My boyfriend and I have been together for two years. He's thirty-three and I'm twenty-eight. We talk about getting married someday, but I'm not really sure he's the right guy for me. My friends tell me that I make too many excuses for his insensitive behavior. They think I would be crazy to marry him and that I really ought to dump him. He's got a lot of good qualities, but maybe they're right. He often forgets to call me when he says he will. He teases me in front of his friends even when I tell him that the things he says hurt my feelings. And he often tells me I'm too insecure and should "lighten up." I know I sometimes take things too seriously, but couldn't he treat me with a little more kindness? What do you think? Y.T.

Dear Y.T.,

I think it's a step in the right direction to be asking yourself whether he is the best guy for you. Sometimes friends are able to see more clearly the blind spots we may have about ourselves. I'll guess that your friends have your best interest at heart and that they perceive your boyfriend as taking advantage of your kind nature. Ultimately, however, it is you who will suffer if you continue to make excuses for his behavior, especially those things that hurt you. While the behaviors you describe may not bother someone else with the same intensity, you're the one he's chosen to be with. Hence, he should take into account your feelings and, at the very least, be understanding of how you react and willing to modify his behavior.

Other questions you might ask yourself as you process whether to stay with him require that you take a closer look at your own behavior and motivation. For instance, why would you be willing to settle for someone whom you feel isn't kind enough for you? Do you think your expectations are unreasonable? If so, how come? What was your parents' relationship like and how did each of them treat you? Did you grow to accept unkind behavior as par for the course and all you deserve? Are you re-creating something from your childhood?

You might also examine whether you have a pattern of being in relationships with people who are insensitive to your feelings and needs. I'm not concerned so much with the specifics of his behavior as with the fact that you have expressed your feelings to him and he isn't taking you seriously. Have you asked him why he dismisses you? What went on in his previous relationships that made him believe it was okay to disregard his partner's feelings? It's possible that he has dated other women with "thicker skins." On the other hand, they, too, might have been bothered by his behavior but never spoke up about it. His pointing the finger at you, however, as the one who's "too insecure" keeps the focus off of him and puts you in the more vulnerable position. That can't possibly feel good. Yet it remains your job to set better boundaries with him.

Unless your boyfriend can recognize that his behavior is problematic to the relationship, he'll probably resist making any changes. At this point, it sounds like he believes the problem is all yours and that you should be the one to change. I would encourage you to take your feelings very seriously and work out some satisfactory solutions with your own self. If his good qualities by far outweigh the others, maybe you could learn to live with them. However, I would think long and hard about that. If you can't truly come to a place of acceptance, you will most likely develop resentments and lose trust in him. I highly recommend that you seek counseling. Sometimes our loved ones can more easily look at problems with their behavior when pointed out by a neutral party, whereas the same mirror reflected by a mate just breeds defensiveness and resistance. Good luck!

♥ ♥ ♥ ♥ ♥ ♥ ♥ ♥ ♥

Dear Dr. Debra,

My boyfriend is a slob. We've been together for two years, living apart, and he wants to get married. Although I love him, I can't imagine living with him unless he changes his old bachelor habits. Whenever I've tried to talk to him about his messiness, he just laughs and tells me he's a grown man and can keep his place any way he wants. I don't trust that he would be any different even if we were to share the same living space. What should I do? H.P.

Dear H.P.,

Whenever two people have vastly different cleaning habits and expectations, the disparity can create quite a power struggle as time goes on. I would definitely pay attention to his laughing at you. This is a big red flag you better not ignore. It's not a good sign when a partner won't take seriously something that matters to you. It's possible that his laughter is a sign of embarrassment about his lack of tidiness. But as long as he won't come to grips with this as his own problem, then at this point there isn't much room for negotiation. Wise observation on your part: I certainly wouldn't count on his changing at any time in the near future, given the attitude you claim he conveys.

Of course, if he seems like the right guy for you in most other ways, you could work on acceptance and find alternative strategies to cope with his messiness. As long as you can truly give up any expectations of his improving and don't grow to resent him for not changing, then you should be okay. If he eventually does come around, it will be a bonus for you. If you go in the direction of living with him, I suggest you try a cleaning service, if you can afford one, or designate an area he calls his own where he can leave his stuff wherever he chooses. Or you might try organizing a weekly chore party. Make cleaning a fun couple's activity, where you each get a reward from the other for doing your assigned tasks. This would work best if you set up a cleaning schedule where each of you clearly defines what you expect from the other. Do this in writing and create a checklist so that neither of you gets into the role of being the master nag.

What stands out the most to me is that your boyfriend believes he is a grown man. Maybe he's grown in age and size, but he's certainly not grown in maturity. It's one thing to not be compulsively attentive to tidiness and cleanliness. It's another to be a slob. I'm not sure what your definition of a slob is, as this can be very subjective. But, assuming that at the minimum you mean he doesn't even pick up after himself and there is grime on the counters, I would strongly disagree with his assessment of himself. A "grown man" and "slob" do not fit in the same equation. Part of maturity is responsibility, and that means cleaning up one's own mess.

I would guess that your boyfriend is caught in some kind of control issue with you, in which he perceives you as an authority figure who is taking away his freedom to be his own person. He may perceive your disapproval as a threat and may be asserting his right to be himself without being aware of just how childlike his behavior actually is. If this is the case, try to present your complaints in the most understanding way without being condescending. Voice your preferences clearly and assertively and avoid telling him how he "should" behave. Instead, use statements like these. "I would really feel better about our relationship if you would do your share of the cleaning," or "I know we have differences in our cleaning requirements. It would mean so much to me if you would adjust in my direction. I'll adjust on some issue that's really important to you."

Before you approach him, however, make sure that your expectations are reasonable. In other words, if you are a "neat freak," it wouldn't be fair to hold him to the same standards. Regardless, proceed with caution or your life could become one big mess. Good luck!

Dear Dr. Debra,

My boyfriend and I recently moved in together, and we're having difficulty coming to financial arrangements. He makes about four times more money than I do, and our house is not something I could ever afford on my own. I want to live with him but am finding it difficult to make a significant contribution. Financial independence is also very important to me but seems impossible under the circumstances. I find I am spending more than I make to compensate and am accruing debt in the process. What should I do? S.B.

Dear S.B.,

Just to reassure you, many couples today experience difficulties in managing finances. When both partners earn a living, many times they choose to keep their individual finances separate. This is the case both for unmarried couples living together and for married couples. Not that knowing this makes your situation any easier, but sometimes it helps just to see that your challenges may be more common than you think.

I strongly recommend that you talk to your boyfriend about his expectations. Are your attempts to compensate and put yourself in debt based on a real expectation from your boyfriend, or do you compensate because of something you imagine he is thinking? Do you feel inadequate that you cannot contribute in the same way he can? If so, you might be creating your own problem. If your boyfriend does expect you to contribute more than you can afford, however, then you need to express that such an arrangement is neither fair nor possible.

Does your boyfriend own/rent the house, or is your name also on the title/lease? Did the two of you jointly choose this home, or would he have gotten it anyway? If you didn't sign up for it to begin with, don't take on responsibility that isn't yours.

In other words, if he purchased or leased this home without consulting you, then you shouldn't be expected to carry the same obligation that he has taken on.

Next, examine what financial independence means to you. Does it mean you should be able to afford to spend at the same levels that your boyfriend can? If so, why? Be careful not to base your self-worth on how much money you make. If you don't feel worthy of living in a home you couldn't afford on your own, this may be contributing to your distress.

I know I'm asking a lot of questions and giving you a lot to think about. But it's really important for you to explore all angles of this issue. Keep in mind that you don't have to lose your financial independence by living with your boyfriend, even if he contributes more financially. As long as you come up with a contribution that takes into account both of your incomes and expenses, you should be able to work out a fair distribution.

From a practical standpoint, you might consider basing your contribution on a percentage of your take-home earnings, minus your personal necessary expenditures. Let's say that he contributes 50 percent of his net income minus personal necessities. You might offer the same. Even though the actual dollar amount you give is less, your contribution should be valued just as much.

The most important step is to talk to your boyfriend about your concerns. Be careful not to project your own imagined fears and to deal with the real issues at hand. If your boyfriend has unrealistic expectations of what you can afford, let him know how important it is to you that he adjust his thinking to fit your financial reality. Sometimes it really helps to keep track for a month or so of all that you spend toward the house, including things like food, utility bills, rent/mortgage, or cleaning services. Sometimes people are simply unaware of how much daily living actually costs.

Hopefully, your boyfriend will discuss this with you and openly share his own concerns. If you have difficulty coming to a mutually acceptable agreement, consider some form of counseling to help mediate your struggle. But don't despair. Couples often have more difficulty talking about money issues than just about anything else. Good luck, and keep the lines of communication open.

♥ ♥ ♥ ♥ ♥ ♥ ♥ ♥ ♥ .

Dear Dr. Debra,

My last relationship ended three years ago. Since then I've been on a few dates, but mostly I've been hanging out with friends and enjoying my freedom. In the last few months, though, I've been wishing I had someone special to share my life with. I have no idea where to look. I have a pretty solid career, and I'm certainly not looking for a man to take care of me. I really need someone who will respect my independent life. I was pretty messed up after my last relationship and am afraid to ever get that vulnerable again. But at thirty-two, I think it's time I moved forward. Any hints on how to reenter the dating world? J.Q.

Dear J.Q.,

This could be the beginning of a great adventure in your life. Since you don't sound desperate or in any great hurry to meet Mr. Right, take advantage of your opportunity to really choose a good partner for yourself. Allow yourself the time to closely examine what it is you're looking for in a mate. Make a list of your most important nonnegotiable needs. Create a relationship vision where you picture the qualities you're searching for. Make sure you hold reasonable expectations, but don't compromise too much either.

Pay attention to any unfinished business or unhealed wounds you carry from your last relationship. Be especially careful not to determine your readiness for a new relationship based on your age. Relationship readiness has much less to do with chronological age and much more to do with emotional well-being and maturity. In other words, even if you believe you should be moving forward toward a new relationship, if you haven't worked through your previous hurt, you're likely to re-create the same problems and emotional wounds the next time around. Get conscious about your part in why your previous relationship didn't work out and how it affected you. Learn from what went wrong and develop new relational skills if necessary.

Be careful not to equate being single with having freedom and being attached to someone with loss of freedom. When you're with someone with whom you are compatible, you won't be fighting for your right to your own self. You and your mate will find a natural rhythm for separateness and togetherness.

In terms of how to reenter the dating world, there are many resources designed to help singles meet other singles. Some options may be more comfortable for you than others. But unless an option is particularly offensive to you, keep an open mind and try new things. You have to do your homework to help the process move along. You could ask friends to set you up, or you might try a dating service. Join an organization that supports a cause you like. Volunteer for a charity function. Most importantly, get out and do the things you like to do. Make a statement to yourself that you are open to meeting new people and a potential romantic partner.

Try not to get discouraged with the dating process. Sometimes it takes quite a bit of time to meet someone really worth pursuing for a relationship. Try to enjoy the process with less focus on the outcome or goal of finding a mate. There's something to be learned from each experience. Of course, use your common sense and be safe. Have fun and good luck!

♥ ♥ ♥ ♥ ♥ ♥ ♥ ♥ ♥

Dear Dr. Debra,

I've been recently divorced after a fifteen-year marriage. My ex-husband already plans to remarry. I think he was having an affair with her, but when he ended our marriage, he adamantly swore he'd been faithful to me. I have a sick feeling every time I think of him loving someone else. I still don't understand why he left me. What should I do? K.T.

Dear K.T.,

I'm very sorry for your loss. Fifteen years is a long time to spend with someone only to have it not work out. It sounds like you still have a great deal of grieving to do. Since you say that he ended the marriage, I'll assume the divorce wasn't your choice. He had probably already spent time toward the end of the marriage separating from your bond. This may explain why it seems easier for him to move on at this point.

Knowing whether your ex had an affair (and you may never really know for certain) won't make any real difference to your healing. As hard as it may be, you need to work through your wounds—things like betrayal, loss, loneliness, and separation anxiety. You need to enter into the letting-go process. You have no control over what has already happened, but you can take charge of your present life. No amount of dwelling on his possible infidelity will bring him back to you.

I believe the sick feeling you describe comes about when you focus on things you have no control over, like your husband's having left you and his decision to remarry. You can mend your broken heart by moving beyond the experience of feeling victimized. You can take action, today, in service of creating a new relationship with yourself and paving the way for a better relationship with someone else. I recommend that you seek counseling if you have difficulty moving on. While it takes time to heal, and no one can decide for you how long that should take, you need to at least unglue yourself from a hope or illusion that you can change the past. If you get stuck, explore why you won't let go of someone who chooses not to be with you. When you value yourself and believe you deserve love, you won't be able to settle for someone who doesn't cherish you.

♥ ♥ ♥ ♥ ♥ ♥ ♥ ♥ ♥

Dear Dr. Debra,

How can I get my wife to do more of the things that I enjoy doing, like fishing, hiking, or going to the movies? She would just as soon stay in all the time or go shopping. It seems that we have mostly done what she's wanted to do. Whenever I suggest the things that would make me happy, she shows no interest. After ten years, I'm getting tired of doing all the compromising. Please help. H.H.

Dear H.H.,

You may have unknowingly set up this inequity at the beginning of your relationship. Maybe in service of wanting to please her or coming from a place where you didn't feel entitled to express your interest, you haven't effectively communicated your needs. From your letter, I can't tell whether you have talked to your wife about your dissatisfaction or whether you're hoping she'll sense your unhappiness and change on her own. While it would be nice if our partners could successfully antici-pate our needs, it's truly an unrealistic expectation. It works far better to learn how to directly communicate.

Start by telling your wife that you've become resentful of the disparity in compromising. Make sure to include that you love her and don't want the resentment to get in the way of the relationship or your positive feelings toward her. Let her know that she is important to you and that you want to keep her needs in mind, but that you really wish she would more willingly experience with you the things you enjoy. Make room to have a dialogue with her about why she hasn't participated more in your leisure world. Also, be careful to examine your expectations of her and make sure they are reasonable to who she is as a person. For instance, if she were afraid of heights, it wouldn't be reasonable to expect her to go mountain climbing, but maybe you could take a long walk through a park. Changing a dynamic after it's been the norm for ten years may take some time, so try to be patient.

♥ ♥ ♥ ♥ ♥ ♥ ♥ ♥ ♥

Dear Dr. Debra:

I've been married to the same man for over ten years, and we don't have the best communication. I am so tired of having to remind him to help out with our kids. He doesn't seem to have trouble remembering the things he needs to do for himself, but when it comes to my needs, I have to constantly nag him. He then gets upset because my tone of voice isn't too nice. How do I get him to help without being a constant nag? O.T.

Dear O.T.:

Sounds like your frustration and resentment have gotten the best of you. Thus it will be hard to express your needs in a constructive way. Although it certainly won't be easy, I strongly suggest that you try to resolve your resentments by accepting that you cannot change what he hasn't done, but you can learn to be more effective in how you are heard in the present. You need to leave out comments like, "You've never helped me, it's about time you start now." It might work better if you tried something like, "I notice you're not busy right now. I sure would appreciate it if you would help with...."

From the sound of your letter, I suspect you've already tried many approaches to no avail. You probably need to share with your husband how unhappy you are with his behavior. Try not to come from an angry place. Rather, try to express your hurt. It's also equally important to really listen to his point of view. Does he even agree with you that he doesn't help out much? What are his expectations of you? Are you a stay-at-home mom and, if so, have the two of you ever discussed what you each perceive to be your roles? Have you examined your own expectations of him? Are they reasonable? While this isn't justification for his behavior if he truly is neglecting his parental obligations, he may actually believe that he is doing his share.

Unfortunately, most couples don't openly share their expectations because they often don't even know what those expectations are until they find themselves disappointed with each other. Try setting up a schedule with clearly outlined tasks that each of you commit to doing. It's not up to him to read your mind. Don't test him hoping he'll figure out what he's supposed to do. You may each have very different ideas about what needs to get done. Negotiate and be fair. If you can't make headway, please consider couples counseling. Sometimes just some simple feedback from an unbiased source can shake things up enough to break the power struggle. Above all, you can't change someone's behavior, but you can make requests for what you want. Ultimately, if your expectations are reasonable and he remains unresponsive, you'll need to decide how you proceed with the relationship.

♥ ♥ ♥ ♥ ♥ ♥ ♥ ♥ ♥

Dear Dr. Debra,

There's a guy at work I think is really great. We work closely together but in different departments. I think he's single and I'm dying to see if he might be interested in me. But I'm really shy and don't know what he'll think about a woman pursuing him. He seems to like me, but I can't tell whether he's just being friendly or whether he might actually be flirting. Should I ask him out? L.M.

Dear L.M.,

There's certainly nothing wrong with asking a guy out on a date. That, of course, doesn't mean that he'll like it. Some guys think that's really cool, but others think it's still a guy's place to do the asking. What do you think? If you're okay with asking, then go for it. If he's turned off, what have you lost except a bit of pride, maybe? Actually, you gain more than you lose because you discover something about his preferences and find out early on that his style wouldn't work for you. Then again, you might discover that he's thrilled to be asked.

You might try suggesting something casual, like going out to lunch or having coffee after work. Or, if it's appropriate in your work setting, try to get to know him better while working. One word of caution, though. Before pursuing anything, make sure you consider the possible consequences of dating someone you work with. This may or may not pose a problem. Would this be against company policy? Could it potentially jeopardize your job, and, if so, would that be worth it to you? These considerations may seem a bit premature, but I think it's usually better to have at least entertained possible outcomes to avoid the surprise of any negative consequences. Good luck!

♥ ♥ ♥ ♥ ♥ ♥ ♥ ♥ ♥

Dear Dr. Debra,

My boyfriend and I have been together for three years. During the first year he showed great interest in doing lots of activities with me like walking, movies, dinners, bowling, tennis, and golf. Now he seems more interested in being alone and says he needs space. Instead of getting out and doing sports, he seems more content with watching them on television. He doesn't want to break up, but I'm not happy. How do I get him interested in sharing with me again? K.T.

Dear K.T.,

I can understand your disappointment. Lots of questions come to mind. What's been happening in your relationship? Do you talk to him about your concerns, and, if so, do you do it with judgment or with concern? Does he agree that he has changed, and, if so, is he bothered by the change? Or is he only bothered because you're pointing it out to him?

Though I'm not certain of the context of your relationship, he might be depressed and retreating by using television as a way of coping with his distress or escaping life. If this is the case, then you would probably have seen a retreat from friends and family as well as a disinterest in most things he previously enjoyed. If, however, his withdrawal seems specific to your relationship, then he may be shutting down from the intimacy or he may be angry about things concerning you and not know how to address them directly. A third possibility is that you see now what he is really like. What you experienced at the start could have been the "best foot forward syndrome," wherein he wanted to please you and capture your attention. Getting your approval inspired him to be more outgoing. (That, by the way, doesn't mean he consciously set out to deceive you.) I'm sure there are other possible explanations, but those are some pretty good guesses.

Be careful not to take responsibility for his "getting interested again." You can be helpful and instrumental, but you cannot do it for him, especially if he's comfortable where he is and doesn't express interest in changing. Speak to him directly, but when you do, make sure to come from a loving and caring place. If you approach him with hostility or anger, he'll probably shut down even more. Make "I" statements like, "Honey, I notice you've been withdrawn lately. I miss you and feel sad we don't enjoy the things we used to do together. Is there anything I can do to help?" If he's unresponsive to your gestures, you might suggest couples therapy. Your happiness is just as important as his is. If you're not satisfied and he won't make changes, you may need to consider moving on.

Lastly, do your own inventory and take responsibility for whatever might be your part in having created the change in his interest. Have you been critical of him, unresponsive to his needs, or preoccupied? Do you listen to him when he tells you how he feels about things, or do you dismiss him when he differs from you? These are just a few of the questions you need to ask yourself.

Also, please keep in mind that relationships go through many ebbs and flows around connection and disconnection. The key to creating and maintaining a fulfilling relationship is to know yourself as well as possible and to stay open to making changes when whatever you're doing is no longer effective in getting what you want. No matter how badly you want something from someone else, you don't have power over other people's choices or the right to even try to take that power. Make your preferences known, lovingly and kindly, and be the best person you can be to yourself and your mate.

♥ ♥ ♥ ♥ ♥ ♥ ♥ ♥ ♥

Dear Dr. Debra,

Why do men always insist on being in control of the relationship? My friends tell me I keep picking the wrong guys. Are they right? Thanks, M.P.

Dear M.P.,

While I don't agree that the need for control resides solely with the male gender, I'm sorry that this has been your only experience. The need for control has less to do with gender and more to do with avoiding the anxiety we often feel when recognizing how little control we have over anything outside ourselves. Both men and women who haven't made peace with the limits of their own control may demand to be in charge to keep up that illusion of control. People who dominate others are usually quite insecure and vulnerable to anxiety if they relinquish control. People who feel secure don't have a need to control others and are content with mutuality in a relationship.

Maybe your friends are onto something. You might attract men who take control because you don't clearly articulate your own needs, wants, and opinions. Maybe you choose men who dominate because you consciously or unconsciously don't believe you're entitled to take your fair share of space in the relationship. If you do discover that you've been picking the wrong guys, you need to empower yourself by taking ownership of this as a choice and examining why you keep making it. Otherwise, you'll probably keep picking controlling men and continue to feel cheated or disappointed.

Be careful not to confuse strength or confidence with control. Some people will openly assert their own needs and value and embrace yours. I suggest that instead of trying to figure out why men need control, you should use your energy for something you have control over...you.

♥ ♥ ♥ ♥ ♥ ♥ ♥ ♥ ♥

Dear Dr. Debra,

My seven-year-old daughter keeps begging me to get her a puppy. She insists she'll take care of it. I know she means well, but I also know there's no way at her age and with all of her activities that she would be able to live up to her promise. I grew up with lots of animals and I cherish that experience. But while I don't want to deprive her, at this time, I'm not up for taking responsibility for another life. I feel guilty for disappointing her. Any suggestions? R.J.

Dear R.J.,

It's great that you're so aware of your own limitations and reservations. And, of course, it's also very normal for your daughter to believe she's capable of caring for a dog. But I agree she's probably expecting more of herself than she can actually fulfill.

The first step is for you to clearly decide whether getting a pet is at all negotiable. You're the parent, so ultimately you must decide what you're up for while allowing your daughter to have her feelings about your decision. Part of being a parent involves making decisions that sometimes anger or disappoint our children. In this case, I'm certain that your daughter will bounce back, especially if you explain the reasons for your choice.

If your decision is negotiable, then you might consider trying a pet with fewer needs, such as a fish, rabbit, or hamster. If she does well with one of these, maybe she could demonstrate her readiness to take on the responsibility of caring for a dog. Or maybe you could decide on an age when you think she would be ready and define for her what she needs to do to show you that she's capable. It might be fun if you set up an experiment with her where she can really see what's required in caring for a pet. Get her a toy pet and help her make a list and schedule for pet care. Have her play make-believe for a month and see how she does. Be sure not to promise her anything you're going to resent or regret. That would be far more upsetting to her than the disappointment of hearing "no" on the front end.

Dear Dr. Debra,

How do I get my man to listen to what I need (sexually) without hurting his feelings? Whenever I've tried, he shuts down and it seems to make things worse. Please help. L.F.

Dear L.F.,

People can often be quite sensitive and vulnerable around issues of sexuality. And this often leads people to become defensive. But if you silence yourself because of your partner's reaction, you deny yourself deserved satisfaction. With this cycle, you run the risk of becoming resentful or withdrawn and become more likely to eventually seek your pleasure elsewhere. You're better off continuing to speak up and allowing your partner to struggle through his own hurt. Hurt feelings never destroyed anyone. He really doesn't need protection from them even though he may find his feelings to be uncomfortable.

Though I don't know how you have already approached him, here are a few suggestions that might yield a better result. Try letting him know you would like to talk about your sexual intimacy so you both can continue to learn about what pleases each other. (Do this at a time when you are both relaxed and feeling close, not right after you feel disappointed.) Let him know all the ways you enjoy him, like how he touches you, kisses you, or nibbles on your ear. Reassure him that we are complicated creatures and you do not expect that he know how you like to be pleased without giving him the specific information. Stay away from negative or critical language and keep it positive, such as, "I would really be turned on if we tried...." Show him by example what you like, and invite him to do the same. Try to keep it playful. Make sure to acknowledge him when he's on the right track. If in the end he's still insulted or unresponsive, you'll need to decide whether to further pursue the relationship or whether it might be better to put your energy elsewhere. Only you can decide what you are willing to compromise.

♥ ♥ ♥ ♥ ♥ ♥ ♥ ♥ ♥

Dear Dr. Debra,

I've been dating this guy for two years. I'm twenty-four and he's twenty-eight. We both have stable jobs. He says he loves me, but he often seems preoccupied with other things and doesn't focus enough attention on me. He says I'm too needy and shouldn't make problems out of nothing. Is it unreasonable to want him to get totally into the moment with me? How would I get him to do that? Thanks, B.L.

Dear B.L.,

I'm always suspicious when someone labels another person as too needy. It may be true that you need more from your partner than he is able or willing to provide, but that doesn't make you objectively too needy. You may need to find a better way to negotiate with him for what you need. If others also think of you as too needy, you might want to examine whether you are picking relationships with people who don't have enough to offer you or whether you actually do expect more than what a partner can reasonably provide. In either case, you might need to heal from some unresolved childhood wounds before you can have a healthy intimate relationship. (By the way, most of us have unfinished business from past relationships that interferes with getting the love we want.)

Assuming that you're being realistic, ask him to stop calling you needy and tell him you understand that your needs may be too much for him. Be specific about what you want and present your requests as "I would really like..." rather than "You never...." He may not understand how to focus exclusively on you. Create a picture for him. For example, you might say,

"Let's have dinner out and talk about our future dreams together." Or you could try joining him in whatever you think distracts him from you. Tell him you would love to spend an hour talking about whatever he chooses and then ask him to do the same for you. Massages, yoga, or other mind-freeing activities probably wouldn't hurt.

If you can't make headway on these issues, consider couples counseling before getting more seriously involved. As life becomes more complicated with more responsibilities, these issues will probably only get worse if not addressed. Good luck!

♥ ♥ ♥ ♥ ♥ ♥ ♥ ♥ ♥

Dear Dr. Debra,

I've been married for two years. I love my husband dearly, but I can't stand my in-laws, especially my mother-in-law. Because they live close by, my husband wants to see them often. They came to our house for Thanksgiving this year, and all they did was complain. I don't mind so much when they're just harping on things in general, but when they start to get personal, I sometimes get really offended. They tell me I'm too skinny and should eat more. I am personally quite satisfied with my weight and the way I eat. They pick on how I've decorated our home and give their "polite" suggestions on how I can improve the appearance of each room. My husband doesn't seemed fazed in the least. He just ignores them. I'm going out of my mind. The thought that they will need to be included in the rest of our holiday gatherings just appalls me. Can I say something to them, or should I just keep my mouth shut? Please help. G.P.

Dear G.P.,

The old in-law problem. It can be a difficult one to resolve. I think your husband has the best attitude, if he truly remains unaffected. While it may not be as easy for you to adopt his stance, I do recommend that you aim for greater neutrality. Even when your in-laws stick their noses into the things you consider personal, you still have the power not to let them get to you.

Something that works pretty well for me when I'm around people who push my buttons is to imagine a protective shield of Plexiglas encasing my body. Create a window that you control, deciding whether it stays open or closed and to what degree. If something comes your way that's unwanted, keep your window tightly shut. If the comments or interactions are benign, you may want to open your window. You will always keep your hand on the lever ready to close the window if necessary, especially when surrounded by people with whom you don't feel particularly safe.

While you may choose to confront your in-laws directly, I think you're better off trying some other more subtle tactics first. Usually people who feel entitled to express their opinions without having been asked don't respond all that well to feedback about their behavior. They may even call you "overly sensitive," in which case you've accomplished nothing other than possibly getting your feelings hurt one more time. However, if you do believe they will respond respectfully to your telling them to please keep their complaints to themselves, then go right ahead.

On a more subtle tone, you might try saying something like, "Thank you very much for your feedback, but I'm quite happy with the way I eat (or how I decorate, etc.)." Or you might say, "Maybe you could write your suggestions down for me. I'll be happy to look them over at some other time." These kinds of responses may be all you need to disarm them and take the wind out of their sails. Who knows? They may pick on you because they get a rise out of you. If you don't give them any ammunition, they may decrease their unsolicited opinions.

I also recommend that you talk to your husband. Let him know how you feel and specify how you plan to approach them. If he thinks you should just ignore them but you don't feel you can, then it's best if you can get his support if you choose to make a more active intervention. Also, you can negotiate with your husband concerning how often you see your in-laws. Maybe some of the time he can entertain them while you go off and do something else.

While I would never recommend that you or anyone engage with people who do harm, sometimes the behavior of others isn't really all that abusive. We just may respond as though we're being harmed because we don't have healthy boundaries to protect ourselves. I'll assume you have an investment in keeping some form of a relationship with your in-laws, even if it's just for the sake of your husband. So before you're too hasty to exclude them from upcoming events, try to do a little work on your own responses. You might be pleasantly surprised how much you can change the impact of an interaction simply by changing your own response to it. Good luck, and happy holidays!

♥ ♥ ♥ ♥ ♥ ♥ ♥ ♥ ♥

Dear Dr. Debra,

My husband and I divorced three years ago. On paper, we share custody of our two children, but in real life my ex rarely shows up when he's supposed to. Sometimes he doesn't even call to say he won't be coming. Sometimes he even shows up unannounced, expecting to take the kids just because it suits his time schedule better. My ten-year-old son gets especially disappointed and actively voices his unhappiness. My fourteen-year-old daughter seems to be less affected, but I know her father's flakiness must be doing some damage even if she doesn't outwardly complain. I've tried to talk to their dad about being consistent, but he just doesn't get it. I'm at my wits' end. I wonder if I should take him back to court to get full custody and get him out of the picture altogether. Or should I keep trying to teach him about his job as a parent? Do you think it's better for my kids to have a piece of a dad or none at all? R.Y.

Dear R.Y.,

My heart truly goes out to you and your kids. Really tough situation you're in. Your ex-husband clearly isn't honoring his commitments and responsibilities as a custodial parent. And his persistent noncompliance with an arrangement I assume he helped create reflects hostility and arrogance. Also, I agree that your daughter probably also suffers some detrimental consequences despite her silence.

When a parent repeatedly disappoints a child and doesn't take any responsibility for his behavior, the child often develops problems with trust and self-worth. And the child may also develop problems being accountable for his own behavior. So it's important to keep observing for signs of distress and try to keep the dialogue open if your children care to talk about their feelings. While you may be quite tempted to bad-mouth their dad and offer character assassinations, I encourage you to refrain from anything other than naming the facts of his behavior. For instance, you might ask, "How do you feel when your dad says he is coming and then doesn't show up?" Then you could empathize with their feelings. Simple acknowledgments like "I understand you're disappointed" or "It's okay to be angry" can sometimes be all children need in the moment to help heal their hurts.

You certainly have every right to take your ex-husband back to court. It's important, however, to consult with an attorney first to see whether it would be worthwhile to do so. Then you also need to consider the expense of doing so, financially as well as emotionally. While it's possible that the threat of court may motivate your ex to rise to the occasion and show some follow-through, I wouldn't count on it. Since history often repeats itself, I would guess that if a court order didn't keep your ex in line the first time around, a new order or a demand to comply with the original may provide little, if any, motivation for behavior change.

It's hard to say what would be better for your particular children—"a piece of a dad or none at all." It certainly sounds like it would be easier for you if he were out of the picture altogether. Then at least you would be fully in charge of providing the routine and schedule that would work for you and your children. I would suggest, however, that you withhold any threats of going back to court unless you will truly do so. Otherwise, your words will lose all of their potential power if the actions don't match.

Try setting firm boundaries with your ex. If it doesn't put you in any legal jeopardy, let him know that if he does not arrive within fifteen minutes of his scheduled time and doesn't call, you cannot guarantee that the children will be available to him. Also, be careful not to put your children in the middle of your battle with your ex.

I imagine you have tried many ways to get him to respect and honor his commitments as a parent. It's important to keep in mind, for your own sanity, that ultimately you have no control over your ex-husband's actions. Eventually, if they haven't already, your children will draw their own conclusions about him, and you can be there to help them sort out their beliefs and feelings. Remind them that their dad's behavior in no way reflects who they are. Tell them often how much you love and cherish them.

FINAL WORDS

I hope you've been able to relate to at least some of these scenarios and can apply some of the solutions or ideas in your own unique life. Try to remember that your journey will take however long it takes. Be loving and patient, and keep finding and using as many resources as possible. People heal primarily through relationships with others. So as tough as it may be at times, hang in there. Continue to pay attention, and value whatever you learn about yourself along the way!

INDEX

About the Author

DEBRA MANDEL, PH.D., is a recognized and respected psychologist. She is an authority in the treatment of people who've suffered childhood mistreatment, eating disorders, depression, anxiety, and relationship problems. She treats individuals, couples, and families from adolescence through geriatric.

Dr. Mandel has given talks to a variety of audiences on many topics related to sensitive hearts. She is a familiar voice in the media, with numerous appearances on Los Angeles radio stations, cable television, and Internet radio. She's been quoted in magazines and has had several articles featured in local newspapers. She writes a regular advice column, "Dear Dr. Debra," for *The Tolucan Times* (a Los Angeles–based community newspaper).

Currently, Dr. Mandel divides her time between two private practices, one in Encino, the other in West Los Angeles. She lives in Los Angeles with her beloved family. You can visit Dr. Mandel online at *www.drdebraonline.com*.